In the
Shaker
Style

In the Shaker Style

Building Furniture
Inspired by the
Shaker Tradition

The Taunton Press

Publisher: Jim Childs

Associate Publisher: Helen Albert

Associate Editor: Jennifer Renjilian

Editorial Assistant: Meredith DeSousa

Copy Editor: Andrew Delohery

Indexer: Harriet Hodges

Designer: Susan Fazekas

Layout Artist: Carol Petro

Taunton
BOOKS & VIDEOS
for fellow enthusiasts

Printed in the United States of America

10 9 8 7 6 5 4 3 2 1

The Taunton Press, Inc., 63 South Main Street, PO Box 5506, Newtown, CT 06470-5506
e-mail: tp@taunton.com

Distributed by Publishers Group West

Library of Congress Cataloging-in-Publication Data:

In the Shaker style : building furniture inspired by the Shaker tradition.
     p. cm.
  Includes index.
  "Information from the pages of Fine woodworking and Home furniture magazines"—Introd.
  ISBN 1-56158-396-0
  1. Furniture making—Amateurs' manuals. 2. Shaker furniture. I. Taunton Press. II. Fine woodworking. III. Home furniture.

TT195 .I5 2001
684.1'04—dc21   00-064776

■ About Your Safety: Working with wood is inherently dangerous. Using hand or power tools improperly or ignoring safety practices can lead to permanent injury or even death. Don't try to perform operations you learn about here (or elsewhere) unless you're certain they are safe for you. If something about an operation doesn't feel right, don't do it. Look for another way. We want you to enjoy the craft, so please keep safety foremost in your mind whenever you're in the shop.

Fancy articles of any kind, or articles which are superfluously finished, trimmed or ornamented, are not suitable for Believers, and may not be used or purchased.

—From the Millenial Laws of 1845

CONTENTS

I t seems somehow ironic in this age of fast computers, Internet communications, robust power tools, and a strong economy that we should be so in love with the furniture that was designed and built more than a century ago by the artisans of a small religious sect. Or maybe it's not so incongruous after all. Perhaps our hurried, complicated, high-tech lives leave us longing for some spiritual simplicity.

The Shakers sought to have their belongings, as well as their souls, reflect the tenets of their religion: simplicity, pacifism, utility, economy, prudence, and a striving for perfection. These beliefs resulted in furniture that had clean lines, lacked ostentatious decoration, and showed great uniformity and attention to detail.

These attributes also appeal to the woodworkers who make furniture in their humble workshops. The Shakers taught them that beauty can be found in the proportions, the clean profiles, the simple joinery, the use of readily available local woods, and the near perfection of a talented craftsman's handwork. While most of today's woodworkers stick closely to authentic historical details, they have adapted these details to forms the Shakers would not recognize, such as coffee tables, display cases, and entertainment centers.

The editors of this book have assembled information from the pages of *Fine Woodworking* and *Home Furniture* magazines to help you explore this handsome furniture. The book is divided into three sections. Part One covers the historical background and hallmarks of Shaker furniture. Part Two contains techniques and projects to get you started making your own Shaker-inspired pieces. Part Three includes inspirational examples made by some of the best artisans now practicing the woodworking craft. I hope the ideas in this book prove as motivational to you as they have been to the woodworking editors here at The Taunton Press. If you are like me, you'll want to head quickly to your shop to start making your own beautiful Shaker-inspired furniture.

—Tim Schreiner, editor of *Fine Woodworking* and former editor of *Home Furniture*

Style & Design

When you think of Shaker furniture you probably think of clean lines and functionality. But there's more to it than that. Many elements make up the Shaker style, and those elements are a reflection of the Shaker lifestyle. The elements apply to their traditional furniture, as well as the well-known Shaker built-ins. Beyond the origins and elements, this section presents some keys to designing in this style that you can apply to your own projects.

JEAN M. BURKS

The Origins of Shaker Furniture

When I started work as the Curator of Collections at Canterbury Shaker Village, in New Hampshire, one of my first jobs was to sort through a building once occupied by a recently deceased Shaker sister. The 6,000-square foot, 22-room building was packed with everything from furniture to thimbles. The furniture was, to my inexperienced eyes, Queen Anne, Chippendale and Federal in style, and it included tables, chests over drawers, and lots of cases of drawers. Due to the similarity to worldly country furniture, I assumed most of it was made outside the community, until I noticed subtle differences in the designs.

To identify the distinctive elements of Shaker design, I learned about their community ideals, their institutional needs and their products. I examined the design and construction of signed Shaker furniture, I read Shaker documents, and I talked to the last remaining Eldresses.

It became clear that although the Shakers lived apart from "the world," as they called nonbelievers, their furniture was not created in a vacuum. No one was born a Shaker—celibacy was considered an important virtue—and early Shaker craftsmen were trained in "the world" before converting to the faith. These cabinetmakers brought their skills, tastes and awareness of current styles with them into the Shaker community and influenced the direction of Shaker design during the 19th century. The Shaker style,

is, then, a result of worldly design traditions inflected with a distinct Shaker sensibility.

Ideologically, the Shakers' religious beliefs required that their products reflect perfection; functionally, their communal society demanded furniture that met the needs of many brothers and sisters.

The spare look of early Shaker furniture comes not only from the Shakers' belief in simplicity, but also from their desire to be practical and efficient. Their furniture had to be easily cleaned, thus potentially dust-catching ornaments were eliminated. The furniture had to be easily moved for dusting, so, for example, beds were made with casters. And the furniture had to be versatile so that several members could work together simultaneously to complete a community work task.

FURNITURE BUILT FOR TWO

Desks in many forms—kneehole, fall-front, slant-front and lift top—were all based on worldly prototypes and were produced at various Shaker communities throughout the nineteenth century. However, these types were adapted to suit the needs of the community business officers, called trustees, who worked in pairs and were responsible for keeping accurate records while conducting affairs with the world. As a result, many desks, like the one in the right photo on p. 8, were designed so that two people could work at them. I found it interesting

DERIVED FROM ENGLISH LAD-DERBACKS, Shaker chairs were lightweight and portable. Woven wool seat tape was removable for washing, and the chairs were often hung upside down so dust wouldn't gather on the seats.

CHIPPENDALE INFLUENCE.
The Shaker desk at right is based on a slant-front design, above, common during the 18th and 19th centuries. Shaker trustees often worked in pairs.

that the interiors of each side of that desk are not identical, but probably customized for the specific Shaker trustees for whom it was built.

Shaker women also worked in pairs at specialized sewing desks that are very close in form to Federal-style ladies' secretaries made at the turn of the 18th century (see the top right photo on p. 9). The Shaker sewing desk, shown on the bottom of p. 9,

was probably designed and built so that it could be pushed back to back with another desk, as shown in the photo at top left on p. 9. Here, the sisters could work face to face in pairs. Perhaps they stored their patterns in the shallow drawers at the top and cut fabric on the extra space-saving board that pulls out in front to increase the work surface.

WOMEN'S FURNITURE. A highly veneered Federal lady's desk, below, was the design influence for a Shaker sewing desk, bottom. The sewing desks were often pushed back to back so that two Shaker sisters could face each other.

LOOKING INTO THE SHAKERS' DRAWERS

Storage units, such as cupboards and cases of drawers gradually assumed their familiar design in "the world" during the 17th and 18th centuries. Most of these had a symmetrical layout of three to seven full-length drawers, and they were designed and built to suit the needs of an individual or a small household.

In contrast, Shaker cases of drawers provided storage space for four to six people who shared a single sleeping space. In this arrangement each member had the use of two or three drawers, resulting in the need to create a massive case of many drawers (see the photo on p. 11).

As a result, Shaker dwelling house and work furniture drawers were customized to house specific items, whether these were different articles of clothing, tools of various sizes, or even herbs and seeds.

Another popular form, the chest over drawer, was made throughout the 18th century in colonial New England, and it served as a model for the Shakers. To this basic

GRADUATED DRAWERS. The Chippendale chest at right served the needs of a single person. The large Shaker cabinet on p. 11 probably served the needs of five or six Shakers. At far right, a Shaker cabinetmaker added an extra drawer to the common chest-over-drawer form.

design, the cabinetmakers at the Harvard, Massachusetts, community added a distinctive underhung drawer below the dovetailed bracket base to provide extra storage for community members (see the top right photo).

STURDY SHAKER TABLES

Historically, long trestle tables were used in medieval monasteries and baronial halls where they were centrally positioned during dining and later dismantled and stowed away after the meal. Although the Shakers adopted the overall length and same basic support system to seat large groups of people, they raised the horizontal stretcher on their tables from floor level to a position beneath the top, which provided stability as well as additional legroom for a large quantity of diners (see the top photo on p. 12).

The trestle tables at the various Shaker communities differed somewhat in the design of their legs, tops and stretchers.

After crawling under many of these tables and looking at the permanent bridle or mortise-and-tenon joints, it was apparent to me that the Shakers' versions are not meant to be disassembled, but used in a permanent location in the dining room.

Smaller Shaker tables come in many styles for a variety of purposes. Perhaps most recognizable are the tripod stands with round top, vase-shaped shaft, cabriole legs and snake feet—a close copy of Queen Anne tables that evolved during the 18th century. With an eye for simplicity and functionality, the Shakers pared down the turning on the pedestal, flattened the legs in cross section and, most importantly, added the distinctive underhung "push-pull" drawer, positioned below the rectangular top (see the left photo on p. 13). The stand and storage unit below could be accessed from either side by two sisters working on their sewing projects simultaneously.

There is No Dirt in Heaven

Trundle beds are low children's beds fitted with casters which allow them to roll underneath another bed for storage. This form was popular in England until the 18th century and was probably the prototype for adult Shaker single beds. The Shakers added wooden wheels, called rollers, which allowed the furniture to be easily moved for sweeping the floor underneath (see the bottom photo on p. 12). The Shakers believed that "there is no dirt in heaven," and they consciously designed their earthly living spaces and their furniture with cleaning in mind.

Even their chairs are designed to be easily cleaned. Shaker side chairs, arm chairs and rocking chairs are based on the early British prototypes of the ladderback style.

A TABLE FOR COMMUNAL DINING. Long, knockdown trestle tables (above) were first used in medieval halls. The Shaker's trestle tables were permanently assembled and had a stretcher close to the tabletop, so as to not interfere with diners' legs.

CHASING DUST BUNNIES. Based on an English trundle bed, the Shaker bed (right) had wheels so that it could be moved around the room to facilitate floor sweeping.

THREE-LEGGED STANDS, like the one above, were popular during the 18th and 19th centuries. The Shakers added a push-pull drawer, left, that was accessible from either side of the table.

English and Shaker chairs have slats wider at the top and narrower at the bottom, turned posts and mushroom-shaped finials.

Shaker chairs are very lightweight, and they were often hung from wall-mounted pegboard to facilitate floor sweeping (see the photo on p. 7). The chairs were always suspended upside down so that dust would not settle on top of the seats.

What appears to be a true Shaker invention is the use of woven woolen tape for seating materials, which was more durable, comfortable and easier to install than the typical cane, rush or splint used by the people in "the world." Fabric seats woven in plain checkerboard or herringbone patterns seem to have been common as early as the 1830s. A further benefit of the tape is that it could be easily removed, washed and reinstalled. Fie, evil dirt!

Worldly design, once adapted from the outside, was passed on from Shaker master craftsman to young adopted and apprenticed children who learned the trade from the inside out. When these young craftsmen became masters in their own right, they perpetuated the design methodology and were responsible for defining the classic Shaker furniture design that we know and recognize today.

CHRIS BECKSVOORT

Elements of the Shaker Style

Woodworking masters Jere Osgood, Sam Maloof and George Nakashima each evolved a style and explored it to its ultimate conclusion, and to hell with what was in vogue. The Shakers did the same thing, continually refining their idiom until they approached perfection, without regard to the latest trend. They developed a style of furniture that blends well and fits comfortably in any type of house. The Shakers went out of their way to eschew fashion: The result is timelessness.

I grew up in a house full of Danish modern furniture, which was, it turns out, heavily influenced by Shaker designs. Like the Danish furniture makers, I fell under the sway of Shaker furniture the moment I discovered it—in my case, during a slide lecture in an architecture appreciation course I took in college. The simplicity and utility of the furniture I saw in the slides stunned me. In the late 1970s, I began restoring Shaker furniture, and much of my own work has been in the Shaker vein ever since. I very seldom reproduce slavishly, but you can look at my work and without batting an eye see its derivation is Shaker.

To make a Shaker-looking piece, adopt a Shaker attitude: Keep it simple in design and materials, make it functional and incorporate authentic details. The details shown on these pages were commonly used by the Shakers until about 1860, after which their furniture began to show the worldly influence of the Victorian style.

The Shakers believed "that which has in itself the highest use possesses the greatest beauty." It took the rest of the world nearly a century to come to the same conclusion, when, in the early 20th century, Louis Sullivan declared "form follows function." But these dictums alone do not lead inevitably to a particular style, much less to a specific set of elements and details. In addition to being inspired by their beliefs, the Shakers and the furniture they made were influenced by their historical context.

In short, the Shakers took the furniture they were familiar with, the local styles from New England to Kentucky, and stripped it of superfluous ornamentation. The Shaker craftsman Orren Haskins (1815-1892) perhaps said it best: "Why patronize the outside world?...We want a good plain substantial Shaker article, yea,

Cherry cupboard
80 in. by 44 in. by 19 in.
Canterbury, New Hampshire
Circa 1850-1900

CROWN MOLDINGS

Moldings along the tops of Shaker case pieces are hard to justify as anything but decorative. Most styles of furniture (and architecture) incorporate moldings or some type of overhang at the top. To the eye, a crown molding or overhang denotes an ending; it is much like a period at the end of a sentence. The Shakers, presumably, were not immune to this near-universal need for closure.

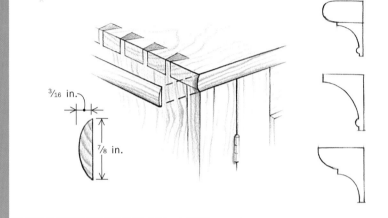

BASE MOLDINGS

Shaker craftsmen used base moldings and profiled bracket bases for protection, not decoration. A rounded or shaped edge is far less prone to splintering or chipping than is a sharp, square corner. This is especially true near the floor, where base molds and brackets are likely to encounter brooms and mops or shoes and boots.

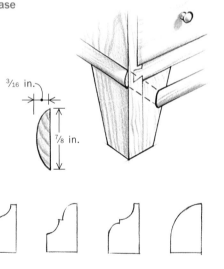

one that bears credit to our profession & tells who and what we are, true and honest before the world, without hypocrisy or any false covering. The world at large can scarcely keep pace with it self in its stiles and fassions which last but a short time, when something still more worthless or absurd takes its place. Let good enough alone, and take good common sense for our guide in all our pursuits, and we are safe within and without."

Shaker furniture, especially from the classic period of 1820 to 1850, contains little in the way of excessive moldings and virtually no carving or veneer. The Shakers favored native materials and were dead set against materials they felt were decadent, such as brass. The Western communities tended to follow the local vernacular style to a much greater degree than their Eastern counterparts. So the Shaker furniture from Ohio and Kentucky appears more ornate.

Some forms of furniture were never built by the Shakers. You will never see Shaker coffee tables, for example, nor tea tables, highboys, pencil-post beds or upholstered pieces. Some furniture companies market these items "in the Shaker style," including improbable pieces such as entertainment centers.

Certain elements appear over and over in Shaker furniture and make sense within the idiom. In striving for a design that remains faithful to the Shaker style, be mindful of their approach—just as you wouldn't build Queen Anne out of poplar, you wouldn't build Shaker out of rosewood. And pay close attention to the details.

DRAWERS

Shaker craftsmen built both flush and lipped drawers. Flush drawers had square edges and fit fully into their openings. Lipped drawers, although more difficult to make, covered the gap around the drawer front to keep out dust. The lips, however, were usually on the top and two sides only. A lip on the bottom was considered too fragile, should the drawer have to be set on the ground. The quarter-round and thumbnail profiles were commonly used on all four edges of lipped drawers. Neither the Shakers nor their worldly contemporaries used the bevel-edged, raised door panel as a drawer front. That design fiasco was perpetrated on consumers by the kitchen-cabinet industry.

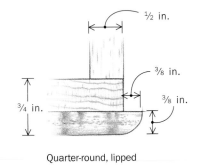

Quarter-round, lipped

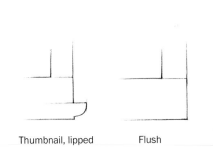

Thumbnail, lipped   Flush

DOOR FRAMES AND PANELS

The doors on early Shaker pieces usually had raised, fielded panels. Over time, however, the raised panel fell out of favor, perhaps because it appeared too decorative or possibly because the shoulder was seen as just another dust collector. In any event, the flat panel ultimately replaced the more traditional raised panel as the first choice of Shaker cabinetmakers. In the transition, the pillow panel, as I call it, was sometimes used. Instead of having a well-defined, shouldered field, the panel was planed on all four edges to fit the groove in the frame. The result was a field that was barely noticeable.

Although square-shouldered door frames were used on occasion, more often than not, the frames featured a quarter-round thumbnail profile along their inside edges. To me, this represents a perfect example of a utilitarian, as opposed to a strictly decorative, molding. Rounded edges along the inside of the door frame are much easier to keep clean than straight, square shoulders.

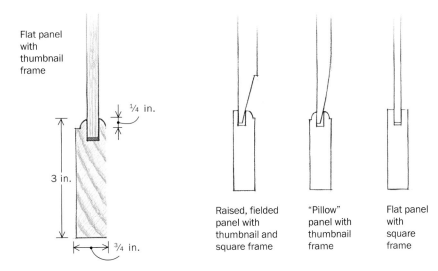

Flat panel with thumbnail frame

¼ in.

3 in.

¾ in.

Raised, fielded panel with thumbnail and square frame

"Pillow" panel with thumbnail frame

Flat panel with square frame

KNOBS

Shaker craftsmen continued the theme of simplicity right down to the knobs. Prior to the 1850s, most Shaker knobs were shopmade, although some early pieces had commercially manufactured porcelain knobs in either white or agate, a marbled brown color. After 1860, manufactured knobs became more and more common.

The typical Shaker knob was a variation of the mushroom form. Sizes ranged from ⅜ in. dia. on tiny desk drawers to 2¼ in. dia. on large built-ins. Knobs up to 1½ in. dia. were typically spindle turned, with either a plain tenon (glued and wedged through the door or drawer front) or a threaded tenon. Larger knobs were usually face turned and attached with steel screws from the inside. Shop-built Shaker knobs were always made of hardwoods, often of a contrasting species to the rest of the piece.

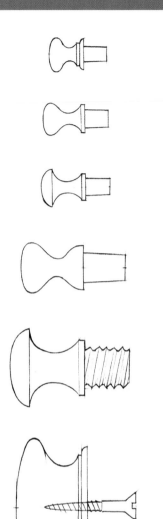

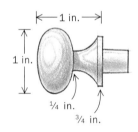

TABLETOP EDGES

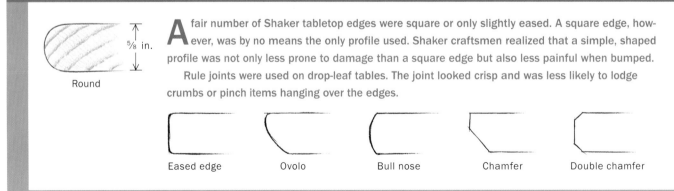

A fair number of Shaker tabletop edges were square or only slightly eased. A square edge, however, was by no means the only profile used. Shaker craftsmen realized that a simple, shaped profile was not only less prone to damage than a square edge but also less painful when bumped.

Rule joints were used on drop-leaf tables. The joint looked crisp and was less likely to lodge crumbs or pinch items hanging over the edges.

Round — ⅝ in.

Eased edge   Ovolo   Bull nose   Chamfer   Double chamfer

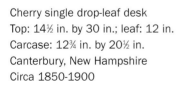

Cherry single drop-leaf desk
Top: 14½ in. by 30 in.; leaf: 12 in.
Carcase: 12¾ in. by 20½ in.
Canterbury, New Hampshire
Circa 1850-1900

LEGS AND TURNINGS

Shaker table legs were, for the most part, quite simple. The double-tapered square leg was by far the most common form. The tapers were cut only on the two inside faces to give the leg a wider, sturdier stance and appearance. Another favorite leg was the straight-turned taper, most often seen on drop-leaf tables. These legs are often splayed a few degrees, because turned tapered legs attached at 90° to the top appear pigeon-toed. Swell tapers were also popular. This form started a bit narrow under the shoulder, then swelled to a maximum diameter at one-quarter to one-half of the way down.

Shaker craftsmen handled the transition from the square area at the top of the leg to the turned portion in several ways. Frequently, they cut the shoulder perfectly square, a 90° cut with a parting tool. An easier, more common transition was the 45° cut, resulting in a rounded shoulder.

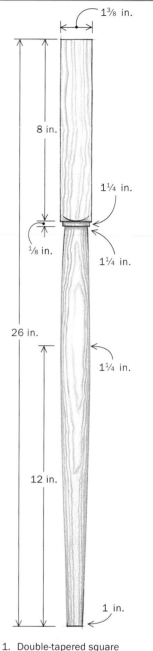

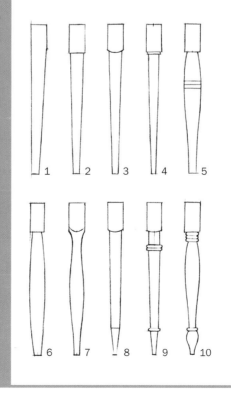

1. Double-tapered square
2. Straight-turned taper with straight shoulder
3. Straight-turned taper with round shoulder
4. Taper with small, flattened ring below square shoulder
5. Swell taper with three scribes
6. Swell taper
7. Swell taper with long, round shoulder
8. Telescope or double taper
9. Straight taper with rings
10. Swell taper with rings and pear foot

TIM RIEMAN

Shaker Built-In Furniture

Considered stark and old-fashioned in its own day, Shaker furniture—I mean the real stuff—now sells readily if dealers can lay their hands on it. Collectors lust after the furniture for its simplicity, its balanced proportions and its honest construction. But you'll need a wrecking bar and a strong back to acquire some of the finest Shaker pieces of all: the built-in cabinets that help give Shaker buildings their graceful architectural flavor.

In nearly endless variation, built-ins are found in each of the 19 Shaker communities that sprang up in New England, New York, Ohio and Kentucky in the late 18th and early 19th centuries. Cabinets like these were rarely found in "the world," as Shakers referred to everything beyond their village gates. Built-ins were used to store everything from chamber pots to out-of-season clothing. And because these cabinets are just as much a part of a building as the roof shingles or window sash, you won't find built-ins in upscale antique stores.

The model for Shaker built-ins may well have been the 18th-century linen chest, a piece of furniture that stood on bracket feet and usually combined a double door over three or four drawers. Built-ins became synonymous with Shaker furniture. In fact, some of the first Shaker pieces of any kind probably were the built-ins found in circa 1790 meetinghouses in Sabbathday Lake, Maine, and Canterbury, New Hampshire.

These simple one- and two-door cupboards were prototypes of the much more complex furniture that would follow.

Once Shakers saw the advantages of built-in furniture, they mined the idea for everything it was worth. They installed the cabinets in offices, hallways, dining rooms, bedrooms and kitchens. Immense built-in storage cabinets went into attics. Shakers also expanded and cultivated the form into complex arrangements of cupboards and drawers. No other craftsmen of the day incorporated cabinets into architectural structures so extensively.

FURNITURE TO SUIT A COMMUNAL LIFESTYLE

We remember the Shakers now mainly by the things they left behind, not by their religious tenets. So it's easy to forget that the great Shaker craftsmen were a celibate, hardworking bunch whose religious observances were so fervent that the Shakers often had hundreds of curious visitors. With the influx of new converts and the growth of Shaker communities, particularly in the early 19th century, scores of new buildings were constructed. The Shakers had set out to create their own heaven on earth.

New residences housed families of 20 to 100 members. Retiring rooms (or bed-

STORAGE THAT'S COMPACT, EFFICIENT. This pine and butternut cabinet in a Hancock, Mass., Shaker retiring room (facing page) contains four cupboards and 10 drawers. It probably served several Shaker brothers or sisters.

IT'S PART OF THE ROOM'S TRIM. Unlike other designers of their day, Shaker craftsmen incorporated cabinets into interior trim, as they did with this shallow dining-room cabinet in the Hancock community.

rooms) on opposite sides of wide hallways commonly housed five or six brothers or sisters. Dining rooms might seat 50 or more. Consequently, kitchens were more on the scale of restaurants than of homes of the day. The requirements for storage were proportionately greater, too. Built-ins helped meet these communal needs. Shakers had, in fact, created a new institutional basis on which they designed furniture.

But why so much emphasis on the built-in? After all, stand-alone furniture would have worked just as well. No one really knows. But themes that run through Shaker beliefs—simplicity, cleanliness, order, industry and perfection—may help explain their devotion to the built-in. Cleanliness may have been at the top of the list, as this piece of advice from church founder Mother Ann Lee suggests: "Clean your room well," she intoned, "for good spirits will not dwell where there is dirt. There is no dirt in heaven."

Built-in cabinetry helped Shakers comply with the edict and conserve floor space at the same time. Because the cabinets stretched from floor to ceiling, they didn't hide the dirt and dust that Shaker sisters worked so hard to eradicate.

REGIONAL DIFFERENCES

For all practical purposes, Shaker built-ins are identical to Shaker freestanding furniture. The obvious difference is that craftsmen often integrated built-ins with trim in the rooms where they were installed, making the cabinets part of the interior architecture. Inside, cabinet sides were usually wide, unfinished planks that supported drawer runners or shelves. Built-ins sometimes had no separate backs, making use instead of previously plastered or unfinished walls.

There probably are more similarities between built-ins from one Shaker community to the next than there are differences. The cabinets are free of the extraneous details that Shakers disliked so much, and the basic proportions of these cabinets seem much the same. But some of the detailing—like the style of door and drawer pulls—and the type of wood that was used showed regional variations.

At the Shaker community at Hancock, Massachusetts, for instance, builders tapered their drawer sides so they were ⁹⁄₁₆ in. thick on the bottom and ⅜ in. thick on the top edge. The thicker bottom edge provided plenty of support for the drawer bottom, but the thinner upper edge of the drawer side didn't look too bulky. Drawers are lipped, and graduated in a manner common to the Shakers but no one else. They are not graduated individually, so that each drawer or row of drawers is slightly narrower than the one below. Instead, they are graduated in groups. In one Hancock community

built-in, for instance, the bottom two drawers are the same height, followed by four drawers slightly smaller and the last two even smaller. This style of grouping drawers in sets is found in many Shaker case pieces as well.

The location of the communities had a lot to do with the choice of woods used for the built-ins. At Hancock, for instance, pine and butternut were commonly available. The wood was often given a mustard-yellow or red wash. Built-ins throughout the main dwelling in Hancock have for the most part

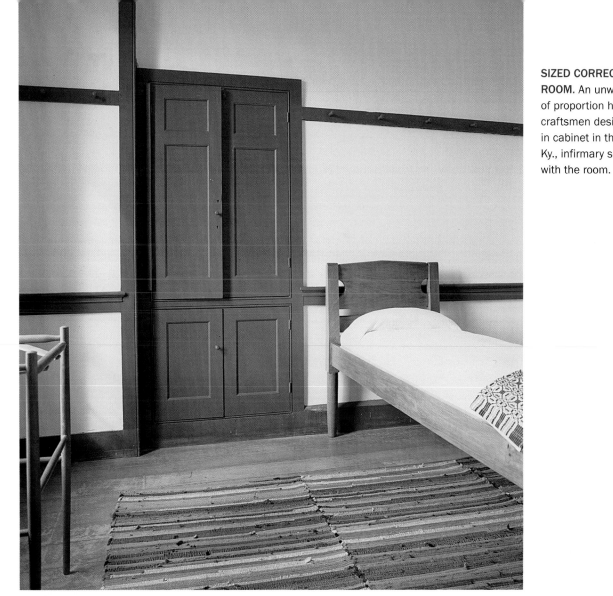

SIZED CORRECTLY FOR THE ROOM. An unwavering sense of proportion helped Shaker craftsmen design a small built-in cabinet in the Pleasant Hill, Ky., infirmary so that it blends with the room.

CABINETS FOR MORE THAN STORAGE. Inventive as well as industrious, Shakers looked for ways to make routine chores less time-consuming. This dining-room built-in in the Hancock, Mass., community houses a dumbwaiter that delivered food from the kitchens one floor below.

been refinished, but they originally showed a vibrant interplay of color.

Because so many Shaker communities sprang up in New England, lots of furniture, including built-in cabinetry, is made of pine. But at the Pleasant Hill community in Kentucky, cherry and walnut were common choices for primary woods because local supplies were so plentiful.

CABINETMAKING ON A GRAND SCALE

Constructing built-ins at a new Shaker residence was no chore for the weak. The brothers who in 1830-1831 put up the main brick dwelling at Hancock tackled a monumental furniture-making venture. The Church Family Dwelling was designed for about 100 brothers and sisters. It provided dining rooms, retiring rooms, a meeting room, and work and storage space. The building, now restored and open to the public, shows a wide range of built-ins, but above all gives a good idea of how busy the carpenters must have been.

Without benefit of routers, belt sanders, biscuit joiners or yellow glue, craftsmen at the Hancock community turned out the work. According to Shaker Elder William Denning, they needed 100 large outside and closet doors, 245 cupboard doors and 369 drawers to complete the building. Built-ins covered a wide range: two units with 28 drawers and four doors in the first attic, numerous single cupboards of various sizes and proportions, tall, slender drawer units in the basement kitchens and even two double-door dumbwaiters used to transfer food from the kitchen to the dining room above (bottom photos, p. 25).

LARGE BUILT-INS FOR CLOTHING

Not even the attic escaped the Shakers' unrelenting desire for order. In fact, some of the largest built-ins of all were attic installations, probably used to store off-season clothing. One of the best known is in an 1837 addition to a building in the Canterbury Shaker community. The third-floor built-ins are distinctive because they are virtually all that you can see in the 35-ft. long room (photo, p. 24). Two long sections include six large units of two doors and 12 drawers each, separated by closet doors.

The pine built-ins partition the room, creating a central hallway between them. Doors provide access to storage behind each unit where the Shakers could stow their winter coats and bedding on racks and pegboards. An ocher or mustard-yellow wash was used to color the pine and basswood casework. Neatly numbered drawer fronts helped the brothers and sisters keep track of their belongings. Small but complex moldings, bolder than those used by most Shaker craftsmen, divide the cupboard space from the drawers below.

Another large but quite different attic built-in is in a third-floor attic at Pleasant Hill (top photo, p. 27). This storage unit looks a lot more like stand-alone furniture than it does the standard Shaker built-in, even though it clearly was not meant to be movable. More closely than other built-ins at Pleasant Hill, this piece shows its Kentucky heritage. The selection of cherry frame-and-panel construction and the absence of a cupboard on top reflect a southern and (at the time) western heritage.

Freestanding cases of drawers from the region were typically of cherry and of a stout, almost over-built, frame-and-panel construction. Corner posts often were well over 2 in. square and were usually supported under the case with turned legs that ranged from simple to complex. True to

form, corner posts on this built-in unit are
2½ in. square, with drawer dividers double-
tenoned into the posts. Its drawers are
finely dovetailed (detail photo, right), and
drawer fronts are unlipped with square
edges flush with the surrounding case.
Finishes were simply varnish, perhaps over a
minimal red wash.

This 45-drawer storage cabinet was built
in three units, each about 10 ft. wide. The
central cabinet went in first, since its top
extends all the way through to walls on each
side of the room. Interestingly, it appears
that the built-in was not part of the original plan of the building because baseboards
and pegboards seem to predate it. The
built-in probably stored off-season clothing.
It was located next to large walk-in storage
rooms with plenty of pegboards. Skylights
directly overhead provided the only light in
the room.

LET NO DRAWER BE OUT OF
PLACE. Deeply grooved from a
century and a half of wear, this
drawer from the attic built-in at
Pleasant Hill carries an identi-
fying number. Corresponding
numbers on the inside edges
of the openings helped
Shakers keep track of the
45 drawers in the unit.

PETER TURNER

Designing on the Go: A Coffee Table Takes Shape

My sister Wendy offered me a deal I couldn't refuse. She'd give me one of her watercolor paintings if I made a worktable for her studio. She sent me a rough sketch showing a long, low table with a shelf beneath the top.

Then I started thinking. Why not turn Wendy's worktable into a prototype for something I could sell as a stock item in my booth at craft shows? Something everyone needs—a coffee table. This barter proved to be the start of a design-and-build process that produced four versions of this Shaker-style coffee table and culminated in the table you see in the front photo. It gracefully serves its purpose and is not difficult to build.

SMALL CHANGES PRODUCE BIG RESULTS

Along the way, I tried three different leg designs, three approaches to the shelf and top construction, and several different dimensions on the top. Wendy's worktable, at 20 in. high, was a little too tall to correspond to most sofas. I lowered the second version to 18 in. and added a 48-in. by 23-in. top. The legs, turned from 1⅜-in. stock, were slightly tapered and ended at ¹⁵⁄₁₆ in. at the floor (see the back table). Both the top and the shelf had breadboard ends. Although very useful, the table's narrow width reminded me of an aircraft carrier, and the legs ended up looking like cigars.

A shortened incarnation, 36 in. by 18 in., with square, tapered legs followed (see the center table). I added a more intricate breadboard design, one with multiple tenons, after I read an article by Garrett Hack describing his approach. That was as much to try a new technique as it was to provide more strength and stability.

But some of these design features made the table too expensive. So to make the table easier and faster to build (and as a

KEEP TRYING. Peter Turner's work on this coffee table began with a request from his sister and a sketch (far left). After several tries, he settled on a graceful design that he could build quickly.

An ample overhang on the top, turned legs and restrained design give this coffee table a decidedly Shaker look. All joinery is mortise and tenon.

2½ in.

55 in.

½ in.

17 in.

18⁹⁄₁₆ in.

FRONT

SIDE

54⅝ in.

14½ in.

SHELF TOP VIEW

result less expensive), I reduced its complexity while retaining its usefulness and grace. Breadboard ends were eliminated on the top and replaced on the shelf with a frame-and-panel design, which I think is easier to make. And along the way, I refined the turned leg from its initial cigar shape to a more delicate form. The first of these simpler versions was 18 in. high with a 48-in. by 18-in. top. I finally settled on a slightly longer version, with a 60-in. by 18-in. top that is ⁹⁄₁₆ in. thick. The shelf is ⅝ in. thick.

SIMPLE CONSTRUCTION COMPLEMENTS THE DESIGN

There aren't many pieces to this table, and it doesn't require much material—in all, about 25 bd. ft. of 4/4 lumber and 4 bd. ft. of 8/4 wood for the legs. I use mortises and tenons to join both the apron pieces and the frame-and-panel shelf to the legs.

I start by turning the legs from 1¼-in.-sq. stock. I'm by no means a master turner, so I use only a few turning tools on the legs: a roughing-out gouge, a skew, a scraper and a parting tool. The gouge does most of the work, and the only tricky part is turning the pommel at the transition where the leg goes from square to round. The danger is chipping out corners of the leg where it remains square. So I use the tip of the skew to make a shallow cut at the transition point (see the top photo on p. 31), then a scraper to round over the corners very gently. The detail I especially like is the ¼-in.-wide collar at the transition from round to square (see the bottom photo on p. 31).

Once the legs are turned, I cut apron mortises in the legs and cut stile mortises in the shelf frame rails using a Multi-Router, which is a router-based joinery tool. But it doesn't matter how you cut the mortises. They could be done with a router, a mortiser, a drill press and chisel, or entirely by hand. I make grooves for the shelf in the

THE TOUGH PART IS THE TRANSITION. The point where the leg turns from square to round is easy to ruin. An initial cut with a skew (left) can prevent chipping. A parting tool (below) helps form the collar.

■ Thinner Is More Graceful

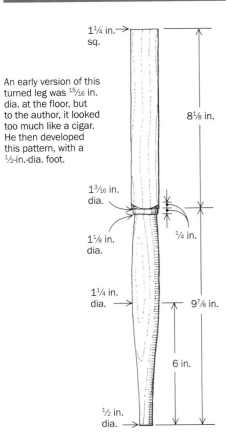

An early version of this turned leg was $^{15}/_{16}$ in. dia. at the floor, but to the author, it looked too much like a cigar. He then developed this pattern, with a $^{1}/_{2}$-in.-dia. foot.

$1^{1}/_{4}$ in. sq.

$8^{1}/_{8}$ in.

$1^{3}/_{16}$ in. dia.

$^{1}/_{4}$ in.

$1^{1}/_{8}$ in. dia.

$1^{1}/_{4}$ in. dia.

$9^{7}/_{8}$ in.

6 in.

$^{1}/_{2}$ in. dia.

DON'T SKIP THE DRY-FIT.
Gluing up all the table parts shouldn't be a nightmare. A dry run pinpoints problems while they can still be corrected.

frame parts on a tablesaw to match the mortises.

When I cut apron and shelf frame tenons, I make sure the length between shoulders on both apron ends and shelf rails is identical so the legs stay square. This means I make the long aprons first and then the shelf, which has a ⅝-in. by ⅝-in. tenon at each corner. I clamp a long apron between two legs and mark shelf mortises in the legs directly from the shelf tenons. Once the shoulder-to-shoulder distance on the shelf is established, I cut the short apron pieces to match.

When fitting the shelf panel, I take the shrinking characteristics of the wood and the time of year into account. Various books provide formulas for figuring out how much each species of wood moves with changes in seasonal humidity.

I fitted the panel in this table in early October, when the weather was still warm, so I guessed the wood was close to its maximum width. The reveals around the edge of the panel are sized accordingly. The panel is flush on both sides of the shelf.

A tenon on each corner of the shelf fits into a corresponding mortise in the leg. I rough out these mortises on the drill press and clean them up with a chisel.

AFTER ASSEMBLY, FINISH UP WITH CITRUS OIL

Final assembly begins with a dry-fit (see the photo on p. 32). Then I glue together the long aprons and legs. The short end aprons and the fully sanded shelf are then glued into place and pinned (I use ⅛-in.-dia. dowel for pins), two pins for each apron joint and one for each shelf joint. To attach the top, I use wooden buttons with tongues that fit biscuit slots cut on the inside edges of the aprons.

After bringing everything along to 320-grit sandpaper, I finish it with three coats of Livos oil, which has a pleasant smell and produces a nice satin sheen.

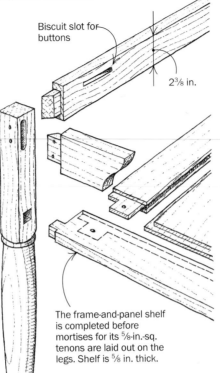

All joinery is mortise and tenon. Apron tenons, ⅜ in. thick and ⅞ in. long, are mitered at the corners.

Biscuit slot for buttons

2⅜ in.

The frame-and-panel shelf is completed before mortises for its ⅝-in.-sq. tenons are laid out on the legs. Shelf is ⅝ in. thick.

■ MAKING IT SHAKER WHEN THE SHAKERS DIDN'T MAKE IT

Can't imagine a living room without a coffee table? The Shakers could. They didn't build coffee tables. To give my design a feeling that is reminiscent of Shaker work, I turned to my reference library (the four books I find most useful are listed here).

If you want to know more about the religious and social basis of Shaker craft, you can start with something called "Orders and Rules of the Church at Mount Lebanon: Millennial Laws of Gospel Statutes & Ordinances." This summary of Shaker habits—described in some of the books I used—was published for church elders in several versions between 1821 and 1887. Laws

covered general approaches to furniture, and they could be very specific: The 1845 laws required beds to be painted green and limited bedroom mirrors to 18 in. by 12 in.

For the design of this table, I looked at photos of Shaker work. The greater the variety and number of photographic examples I absorbed, the stronger my vocabulary became in the elements of form, scale, proportion and balance. This accumulated understanding allowed me to use specific design characteristics in this coffee table. Thin tops, ½ in. or ⅝ in., and ample overhangs, 2 in. to 3 in., on table ends are common on Shaker tables, so I adopted those elements here. The leg transition from square to collar to round came from a Shaker side table

made in Enfield, N.H. Along with sound joinery and little decorative elaboration, the prudent selection of design elements evokes a harmony and balance present in the majority of Shaker work.

My list of most useful books includes:
The Complete Book of Shaker Furniture by Timothy Rieman and Jean Burks (Harry N. Abrams, 1993)
Shop Drawings of Shaker Furniture and Woodenware, Vols. 1, 2, and 3 (The Berkshire Traveller Press, 1973-1977)
The Book of Shaker Furniture by John Kassay (The University of Massachusetts Press, 1980)
Illustrated Guide to Shaker Furniture by Robert Meader (Dover Publications, 1972)

PETER TURNER

A Modern Makeover for a Shaker Linen Press

The flush panels, flared legs and seamless cove of the crown molding give this traditional hutch a somewhat contemporary look, but it is clearly rooted in mid-19th century Shaker design, more specifically the casework of the western Shaker communities. In this piece, I drew on two linen presses built by Shaker furniture makers from Pleasant Hill, Kentucky. The combination of the frame-and-panel construction of the lower case and the dovetailed upper cabinet grew out of these examples.

Reworking the form for a modern setting—a small New York City apartment—

NEW USE FOR AN OLD FORM. Linen presses were used for storing clothing or valuable linen. In this modern adaptation, the form was pressed into service as a dining room hutch (facing page). The customers outfitted one of the drawers with a removable silver tray and used less obtrusive glass shelves, rather than solid wood, in the upper cabinet (right).

HOW TO MAKE THE HARD-WARE DISAPPEAR. Discreet hardware, like these bullet catches and knife hinges, keep the focus on the wood.

was a true collaboration. My customers made a detailed sketch—right down to the knife hinges—loosely based on Shaker forms. Within their guidelines, I put together some sketches of my own.

A wall in their small dining room established the maximum width of the hutch—64 inches—and gave me a place to start, at least for the dimensions. I decided to add a coved crown molding and turned legs, a detail that I found in a book by Ejner Handberg called *Shop Drawings of Shaker Furniture and Woodenware* (Berkshire Traveller Press, 1975). The turned legs would replace the bracket feet in the customers' original drawing.

We exchanged drawings by mail, but it wasn't until later that we settled on the

FOR MORE ON SHAKER DESIGN AND CONSTRUCTION

I leaned heavily on a few helpful references while designing this hutch: The *Complete Book of Shaker Furniture*, by Timothy D. Rieman and Jean M. Burks (Harry Abrams, Inc., 1993) has photographs of two "presses" (pp. 326-327) from Pleasant Hill, Kentucky. For construction details, such as attaching the top case to the bottom (I chose simple cleats), I turned to an article by Ronald Layport in *Fine Woodworking* ("Building an Open Hutch," No. 89, July/August 1991). To cut the cove shape for the crown molding, I used a skewed fence on my tablesaw, a method described by Frank Klausz III in his *Fine Woodworking* article ("Coves Cut on the Tablesaw," No. 102, Sept./Oct. 1993).

details. Motorcycling through Maine on vacation, the customers decided to stop by my shop to discuss revisions. Because the hutch was to share the room with a dining set they had made for them in Germany, we revisited the leg design. We replaced the turned legs I had suggested with curved, tapered ones that relate to the dining table and chairs.

The flared legs seem to balance the shape of the crown molding, which I had left flush with the side of the top to create an uninterrupted line. The flat, flush panels—both inside the cabinet and out, front and back—are a personal preference. To me, the panels and the unobtrusive hardware contribute to the cleanliness and simplicity of the facade.

The cherry hutch has maple drawers and wedged-and-tenoned pulls of sustainably harvested granadillo from Mexico.

ECONOMY OF LINE. Building on the orderliness of Shaker design, the author added inset doors and flush panels, giving the design a more contemporary facade.

ADDING FLARE TO THE FEET

The curved, tapered legs balance the deep cove of the crown molding. The rear legs only curve to the side so that the back of the hutch can be placed against a wall, while the front legs flare to the side and front.

61 in.

17 in.

55 in.

52 in.

14 in.

60 in.

37 in.

57 in.

20 in.

8 in.

Projects & Techniques

N ow that you've
learned about the
hallmarks of the
style, we'll take a look at
some creative projects.
Whether you want to build
a revolving chair, a sewing
stand, or a workbench,
you'll find what you're looking for in this section. At
the end of the section, we'll

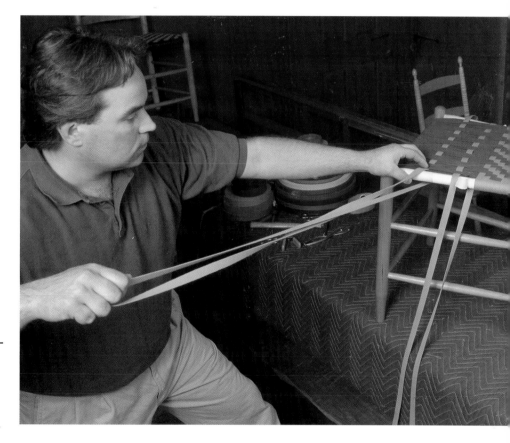

address some techniques common to Shaker furniture. You can apply these techniques
to any of the projects here, or whatever you design on your own.

MARIO RODRIGUEZ

The Shaker Revolver

Back in 1986, I was lucky enough to attend a New York exhibition of Shaker furniture that had been gathered from private collections. One of the pieces was an unusual rotating stool called a revolver (see the photo at right). Like most Shaker furniture, the design was clean and spare, and the stool had been made with the Shaker's remarkable craftsmanship. Unlike most Shaker furniture, this stool was a completely original design. It was a versatile piece of 19th-century workplace furniture well-suited to any 20th-century interior.

I put the stool out of my mind until recently, when I needed a compact home-office stool—something small enough to slip under a desktop yet large enough to be comfortable for more than a few minutes at a time. I didn't want some chrome and fabric contraption, so the revolver seemed like a good answer.

Although the stool requires both turning and steam-bending, it's still fairly simple to make. The only sticking point seemed to be a hardware problem: Where was I going to get the parts to make the rotating mechanism that connects the base to the seat? After a few failed trips to local hardware suppliers, I found Jeremy Lebensohn of Studio dell'Arte, who constructed a working mechanism from odds and ends he uses to fabricate staging platforms for theaters. His design is simple: a ¼-in.-thick steel plate,

6 in. sq., welded to a 10-in. length of ⅝-in.-dia. Acme threaded rod. The rod passes through a 1-in.-sq. tapped block of steel that controls the vertical travel of the plate. Studio dell'Arte (Pier 63, North River, New York, NY 10011; 212-727-2914) will sell this mechanism for $40, which includes shipping charges. You could also check with a machine shop in your area.

A LOOK AT THE BASIC PARTS

Each of the stool's parts requires different skills. The base is made up of two identical arches of 3-in.-thick solid walnut joined with a half-lap joint at the center and secured to the bottom of the pedestal with four #10 flat-head screws. The pedestal is a two-part lamination that holds the tapped block of the mechanism captive. The seat is simply a round block gently dished in the center. After being turned to a perfect taper on the lathe, the spindles are steam-bent to a subtle curve. The back rail crowns the revolver with a gentle curve, steam-bent to a 9¼-in. radius.

I made my stool of walnut. Shaker versions usually were a combination of several different woods: hickory for the spindles and rail, cherry or maple for the pedestal and base, and pine for the seat. These everyday stools were constructed from whatever was handy. Whichever wood you choose for

This reproduction revolver looks right at home in the old Ministry Shop on the grounds of Hancock Shaker Village in Pittsfield, Mass.

Shape and Size of Turned Seat

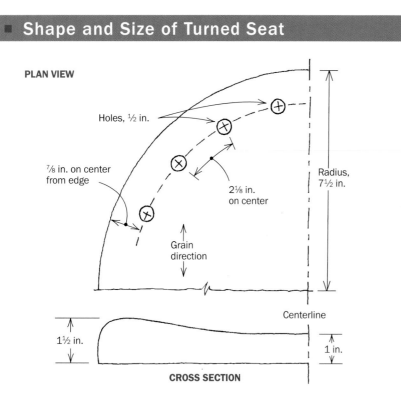

PLAN VIEW

Holes, ½ in.

⅞ in. on center
from edge

2⅛ in.
on center

Grain
direction

Radius,
7½ in.

Centerline

1½ in.

1 in.

CROSS SECTION

Back Rail

Blank is cut to 21 in. long and then turned on a lathe
before steam-bending.

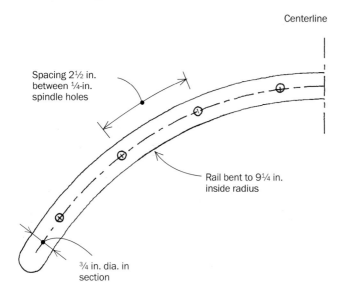

Centerline

Spacing 2½ in.
between ¼-in.
spindle holes

Rail bent to 9¼ in.
inside radius

¾ in. dia. in
section

the bent parts, it must be green (freshly harvested) to ensure successful bending. Kiln-dried wood does not bend easily and will spring back more readily.

TURNING THE SEAT, SPINDLES AND RAIL

The seat was glued up from two pieces of walnut, 1½ in. thick, to form a 16-in.-dia. blank. To make turning easier, I bandsawed the shape to within ¼ in. of the finished 15 in. dia. and mounted the blank on my lathe with a 6-in.-dia. faceplate.

When turning large pieces of wood on a lathe, it's a good idea to turn your project at a slow speed (I set my lathe speed at 600 rpm). Turning at a high speed will cause excessive vibration, posing risks to both you and your work. The shape of the seat is fairly straightforward (see the top left drawing). It has a rounded top edge and a ½-in.-deep depression in the center. After turning the seat, I sanded it to 400-grit at about 1,725 rpm.

Both the spindles and the rail should be turned before they are bent. A common problem in turning thin pieces is whip, which occurs when a workpiece vibrates and moves away from the cutting edge as force is applied. Sometimes the tool will slip between the workpiece and the tool rest, either deforming the spindle or popping it free. Once these pieces are damaged in any way, they must be discarded.

An easier way to turn the spindles is to use a block plane on the lathe (see the photo on p. 43). This technique leaves a smooth and even taper. I made sure to turn the top and bottom tenons slightly over-sized to allow for shrinkage when the parts dried. Later, I shaved them down with a coarse file for a tight fit.

The back rail, at 21 in. long, required the use of a steady tool rest to reduce whip. If you don't have one, the back rail can be steamed square, and after bending, shaped with a ⅜-in. quarter-rounding bit mounted in a router. It's a good idea to prepare the back rail bending blank with a few extra inches at each end: this will give you leverage during bending and minimize kinking.

GLUE UP THE PEDESTAL, AND THEN TURN TO SHAPE

The pedestal is made from two pieces of 2-in. by 4-in. rough walnut. I plowed a ⅝-in. channel down the center of each piece on the tablesaw for the threaded rod. Then I marked out the position of the tapped block and chiseled out a mortise to receive it (see the top photo on p. 44). This part had to fit perfectly—any slop was eliminated with shims. Once the block fit, I dry-clamped the two halves together and engaged the threaded rod to make sure the alignment was perfect and the threaded rod didn't bind. Care and caution now saves work later on. The two pieces may now be glued together with the threaded rod in place.

To turn the laminated pedestal to the final vase shape, I added pine shoes at each end (see the bottom photo on p. 44). With the center channel cut, I needed a solid surface for mounting between centers on the lathe. I turned the top of the pedestal down to a 1⅞ in. dia. to receive a brass ferrule, which strengthens and decorates the slender neck (I used a short length of brass pipe that I got from Space Surplus Metals, 325 Church St., New York, NY 10013; 212-966-4358). Then I mounted a 1¼-in.-long piece of the pipe over the live tailstock center and checked the fit periodically as I turned the neck. I left the last ¼ in. of the pedestal neck a little oversized and tapped the ferrule into place. Later, I set a countersunk #4 brass screw to hold it secure.

So the rod wouldn't wear out the wood in the neck, I used a ¼-in. chisel to clean out the top of the plowed channel and hammered home a ¾-in.-dia. by ½-in.-long flush copper bushing (available from any plumbing-supply dealer).

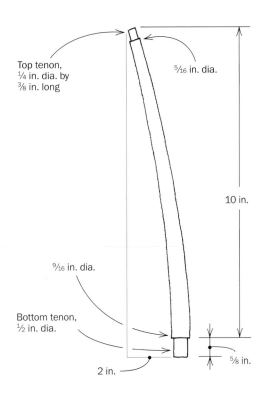

Top tenon, ¼ in. dia. by ⅜ in. long

⁵⁄₁₆ in. dia.

10 in.

⁹⁄₁₆ in. dia.

Bottom tenon, ½ in. dia.

2 in.

⅝ in.

ROUGH OUT THE SPINDLES with a gouge, and clean them up with a block plane. Cut the tenons with a parting tool.

THE TAPPED STEEL BLOCK, buried in the glued-up pedestal, accepts the threaded rod attached to the seat bottom.

SCRAP PINE SHOES MAKE TURNING POSSIBLE. Take care placing the screws, so they won't interfere with turning tools.

SECTION THROUGH PEDESTAL

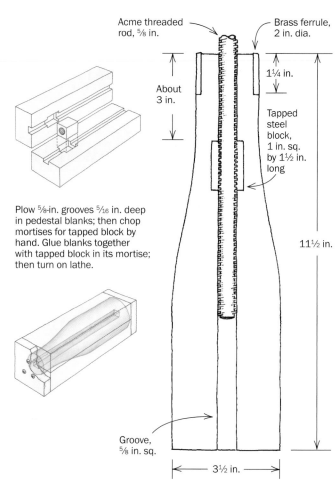

Acme threaded rod, ⅝ in.

Brass ferrule, 2 in. dia.

About 3 in.

1¼ in.

Tapped steel block, 1 in. sq. by 1½ in. long

Plow ⅝-in. grooves ⁵⁄₁₆ in. deep in pedestal blanks; then chop mortises for tapped block by hand. Glue blanks together with tapped block in its mortise; then turn on lathe.

11½ in.

Groove, ⅝ in. sq.

3½ in.

BUILDING THE BASE WITH A HALF-LAP JOINT

For the arches, I used 3-in.-thick solid walnut and oriented the grain lengthwise, like the original Shaker stool. Initially, I was concerned that any weight placed on the arches might cause the short-grained sections to split, but this construction technique was used by the Shakers. Many of their stools have survived, and mine hasn't split either.

The two legs are cut with a half-lap joint at the center. Because the legs taper in two planes, the sequence of cuts is important. I cut out the silhouette first and marked a centerline and a 4-in.-wide section for the half lap (see the drawing on p. 45). One arch was marked topside for the cut, the other on the underside of the curve. After laying out my joint on both pieces, I rough cut each half on the bandsaw by making multiple cuts to a depth equal to half the thickness of the arch, but just shy of my scribed lines. Then I chiseled out the waste and used a shoulder plane to clean up everything for a perfect fit (see the top photo on p. 45).

With the half-lap joint cut, I laid out the taper on the arches and cut them on the bandsaw. All of the curved surfaces, both concave and convex, were cleaned up with a

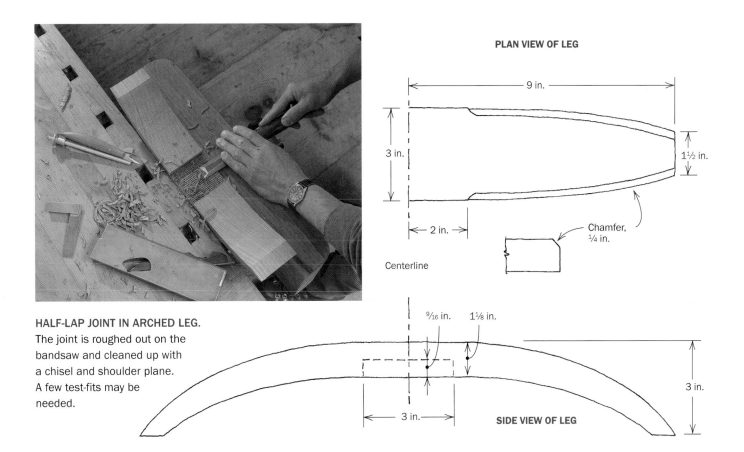

PLAN VIEW OF LEG

9 in.

3 in.

1½ in.

2 in.

Centerline

Chamfer,
¼ in.

HALF-LAP JOINT IN ARCHED LEG.
The joint is roughed out on the
bandsaw and cleaned up with
a chisel and shoulder plane.
A few test-fits may be
needed.

⁹⁄₁₆ in.

1⅛ in.

3 in.

3 in.

SIDE VIEW OF LEG

BACK-RAIL DRILLING JIG. Worth the time spent
making it, this jig guides the drill at just the
right angle for each hole. To keep the depth of
all the holes consistent, you might want to put a
piece of masking tape on the drill bit as a
stop guide.

Bends for this stool are mild and easy to produce, but you'll need some sort of steam-box. I use a fairly large one made of 6-in. PVC pipe, 60 in. long, mounted on a plywood cradle. But for a small, one-time project like this, I'd recommend constructing a small plywood box. A commercial wallpaper steamer, which can be rented from paint stores or rental centers, produces the steam.

The jig for the back rail (see the photo below) is a design based on one I use for Windsor chairmaking. It consists of a ¾-in. plywood form mounted to a backing board. Around the form, I drill 1-in.-dia. holes to accommodate the pegs and wedges that hold the steam-bent blank in place. I cut the pegs from dowels and the wedges from shop scraps.

I used a jig for the spindles to bend them all at once. I glued up pieces of scrap lumber to make an arched form. The bottom tenons fit into holes at the base of the arch. The top tenons are clamped down and held by a plunger.

The pieces are slender and require no more than 30 minutes in the steambox. When removing parts from the box, I always use gloves because the steam is hot enough to burn hands and forearms. I leave the steamed pieces in their jigs about five days, so they will retain their curved shape and not spring back. When dry, I clean them with 120-grit sandpaper.

spokeshave, files and a cabinet scraper. I finished off the curved arches with chamfered top edges.

JOINING THE SEAT AND THE RAIL

The position of the holes for spindle tenons on both the underside of the back rail and the perimeter of the seat are important. Properly placed, the spindles enhance the stool's grace and delicate beauty. If not, the stool will look lopsided and unbalanced.

There are eight holes, spaced $2\frac{1}{8}$ in. apart, bored on a drill press at 90° into the top of the seat. The holes in the rail are drilled at two angles—75° for the four center holes and 7° for the four outside holes. This fine degree of change helps to make the spindles fit right and look good. I made a drilling jig based on a 9¼-in. radius to help locate my holes at the correct angle (see the bottom photo on p. 45).

ASSEMBLING AND FINISHING THE STOOL

It's always a good idea to dry-assemble any project before glue-up. In the construction of the Shaker revolver, it's critical. After the rail and spindles fit correctly, I drew registration marks on masking tape applied to both spindles and seat, so I could reassemble the parts exactly the same way later. When I went to glue-up, I simply lined up the marks on the masking tape.

Many of us have horrible memories of using shellac in junior high school shop class. It was thick and pungent, difficult to brush on and left awful streak marks. It never seemed to dry. I overcame these problems when I learned to mix my own, using fresh shellac flakes and a good-quality solvent blended to a water-like consistency. Such a thinned mixture makes shellac a versatile and attractive finish, and that's what I used for the stool, adding a little red pigment to warm up the color of the walnut. After four coats of shellac, I applied two coats of furniture wax.

RAIL-BENDING JIG. Four hands are better than two for forcing the steamed rail into shape. The author is assisted by Les Katz, one of his students. Wedges hammered between the plywood form and the wooden pegs hold the rail tightly in place.

ROBERT TREANOR

Shaker Sewing Stand Remains Stylish, Practical

S haker sewing stands have a simplicity and a charm that few other pieces of furniture can match. Although I don't sew, and have buttonless shirts to prove it, I am drawn to these small stands. And that's not just because I like Shaker furniture. The stand's convenient size and two-way drawer (see the top drawing on p. 48) make it useful for any household—as an end table, a night stand or especially as a hall table. Because the table is small, it will fit in almost any entryway, providing a place to drop the mail and your keys.

Most of us are familiar with the Shaker candle stands that have round tops. In Shaker communities, round stands were great for candles, but their tops didn't hold much else. Shaker craftsmen sometimes substituted rectangular tops for the round ones and suspended a drawer or two under the top to provide additional storage. These tripod stands usually are called sewing stands, although their main purpose is debatable.

Several versions of sewing stands with under-slung drawers evolved (see the story on p. 53). The style I like best has a single drawer and cabriole-style (snake) legs, as shown in the photo at right. I built this stand mostly from cherry, with a few pine parts. Similar stands are attributed to the Hancock Shaker community in western Massachusetts and are, arguably, the most elegant. The height usually is about 26 in.

The legs on the original stand, on which my piece is based, are tenoned into the

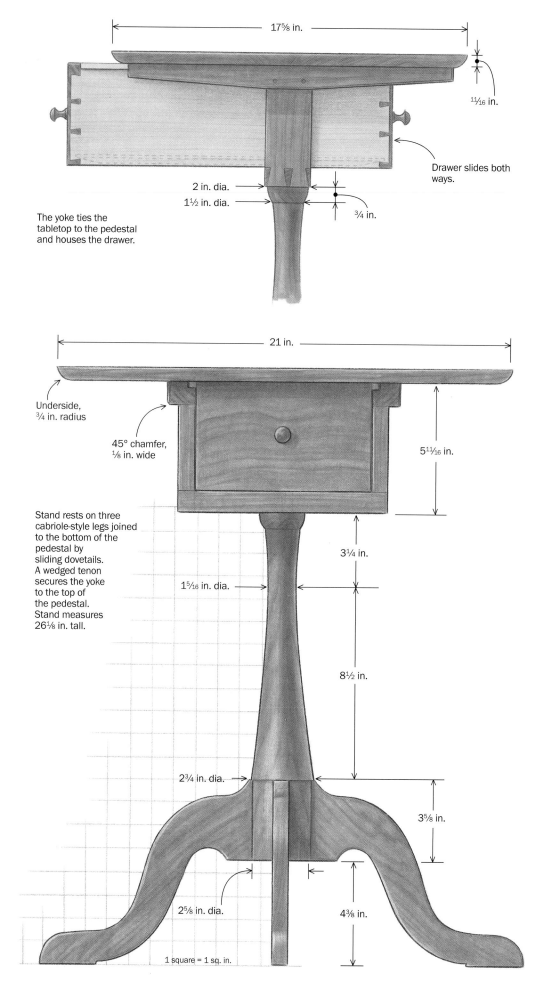

17⁵⁄₈ in.

¹¹⁄₁₆ in.

The yoke ties the tabletop to the pedestal and houses the drawer.

2 in. dia.

1½ in. dia.

¾ in.

Drawer slides both ways.

21 in.

Underside, ¾ in. radius

45° chamfer, ⅛ in. wide

5¹¹⁄₁₆ in.

Stand rests on three cabriole-style legs joined to the bottom of the pedestal by sliding dovetails. A wedged tenon secures the yoke to the top of the pedestal. Stand measures 26⅛ in. tall.

3¼ in.

1⁵⁄₁₆ in. dia.

8½ in.

2¾ in. dia.

3⁵⁄₈ in.

2⅝ in. dia.

4³⁄₈ in.

1 square = 1 sq. in.

turned pedestal (a common feature of Hancock stands). The legs on my stand are joined to the pedestal by sliding dovetails. This joinery adds strength to the piece. Some original stands were built this way, and to further strengthen the connection, a metal plate (known as a spider) was secured to the bottom of the pedestal. I omitted the spider on my stand. The bottom drawing at left shows the patterns for the legs and the pedestal. I cut the leg dovetails on a router table. For the pedestal grooves, I use a jig and a hand-held router with the pedestal still mounted on the lathe, as shown in the bottom photo on p. 50.

THE YOKE UNITES THE TOP, THE DRAWER AND THE PEDESTAL

The tabletop on my stand is 21 in. wide by 17⅝ in., front to back. I edge-joined the top from two 4/4 boards. After glue-up, I planed the top to 1¹⁄₁₆ in. thick, and I shaped the edges all around using a ¾-in. roundover bit in my router. The radius is clipped because of the table thickness, but this slightly flattened round is intentional.

The U-shaped yoke that houses the drawer and attaches the top to the base distinguishes this stand from those with two drawers. The two vertical members of the yoke are joined to the crosspiece with

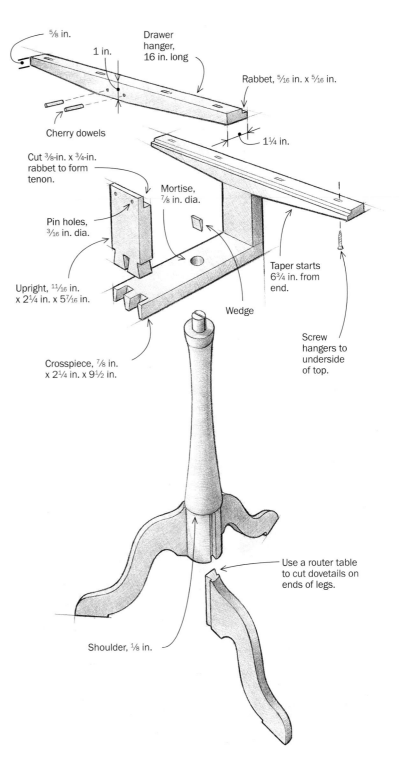

5/8 in.

1 in.

Drawer hanger, 16 in. long

Rabbet, 5/16 in. x 5/16 in.

Cherry dowels

1¼ in.

Cut ⅜-in. x ¾-in. rabbet to form tenon.

Mortise, ⅞ in. dia.

Pin holes, ³⁄₁₆ in. dia.

Upright, ¹¹⁄₁₆ in. x 2¼ in. x 5⁷⁄₁₆ in.

Taper starts 6¾ in. from end.

Wedge

Screw hangers to underside of top.

Crosspiece, ⅞ in. x 2¼ in. x 9½ in.

Use a router table to cut dovetails on ends of legs.

Shoulder, ⅛ in.

■ Legs-to-Base Detail (Bottom View)

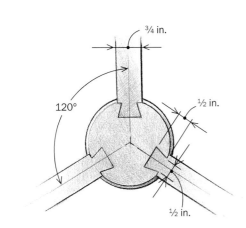

¾ in.

120°

½ in.

½ in.

GLUE AND INSERT A WEDGE IN THE SLOTTED TENON to secure the yoke to the pedestal. Orient the wedge perpendicular to the crosspiece's grain to prevent splitting.

A GUIDE BLOCK IMPROVES ACCURACY. When chopping the through dovetails in the crosspiece, the author uses a block of wood to guide his chisel. The crosspiece forms the bottom of the U-shaped yoke.

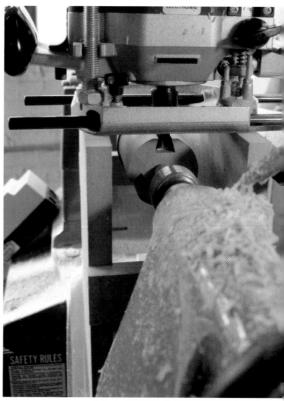

ROUTER JIG CUTS SLIDING DOVETAIL SOCKETS. With the pedestal still mounted on the lathe, use a router to cut sockets for the leg dovetails.

ASSEMBLE THE DRAWER WITH THE BEVEL DOWN. The pine bottom floats in grooves in the pine sides and in the cherry drawer fronts.

through dovetails. The yoke could be joined with a single dovetail, but the original stand had twin dovetails. I used one in the middle and a half pin at each end.

Dovetailing the crosspiece to the uprights

I laid out the dovetail pins on the horizontal crosspiece. For accuracy, I cut the pins with a *dozuki* (a Japanese crosscut saw) and a chisel. When I chopped out the waste at the deep part of the pins, I guided the chisel against a square block clamped to the top of the work (see the far left photo on the facing page).

I lay out the tails on the uprights of the yoke using the pins as a pattern. Just as with the pins, I carefully saw the tails and

chop out the waste. Ideally, the joint will fit right from the saw. But a little paring with a chisel is often needed.

Tenoning the yoke to the pedestal

The yoke crosspiece is attached to the stand's base by a turned tenon on top of the pedestal. I sized the tenon while the pedestal was still on the lathe. I like to rough out the tenon diameter so it's slightly greater than the finished one. Then, using a gouge (you could also use a skew), I slowly trimmed the tenon down to size, stopping the lathe frequently and checking the tenon diameter with a dial caliper.

I bored the hole in the crosspiece and sawed a slot in the tenon before the yoke was assembled. Then I assembled the yoke, placed it on the pedestal and drove a wedge, wet with glue, into the tenon to lock the yoke in place (see the top right photo on p. 50). To avoid splitting the crosspiece, I oriented the wedge perpendicular to the grain.

THE DRAWER IS SUSPENDED AND GUIDED BY TWO HANGERS

A ¼-in. by ¾-in. runner was glued and nailed to the top of each drawer side. The runners guide the drawer in two L-shaped hangers that connect the yoke and tabletop. The hangers, tapered gently at each end, have rabbets cut in the upper inside edges to support the drawer. Each hanger is attached to the underside of the top with four screws. I counterbored the slotted holes in the hangers to recess the round screw heads. To break the hard edges of the hangers, I used a spokeshave to make a ⅛-in., 45° chamfer around the outside.

The uprights are joined to the center of the hangers with pinned tenons (see the right drawing on p. 49). It's best to cut the tenons before you dovetail the other ends of the uprights. The stand that inspired mine has two pins at each juncture, which suggests that double tenons were used. I used single tenons, but I matched the look by pinning each tenon with two ³⁄₁₆-in. cherry dowels.

I joined the drawer sides and fronts using half-blind dovetails. The original stand's drawer had through-dovetailed corners, but I opted for half-blind dovetails because I think their functional, understated look goes better with the nature of this stand. The drawer bottom is let into a groove all around the inside, frame-and-panel fashion (see the photo on p. 51). The pulls, turned with integral tenons, are affixed to the two fronts with wedges from the inside. The drawer can be opened from either end. This push-me/pull-you orientation may be unique to Shaker furniture. Regardless, it makes the stand more interesting and useful.

■ Drawer Detail

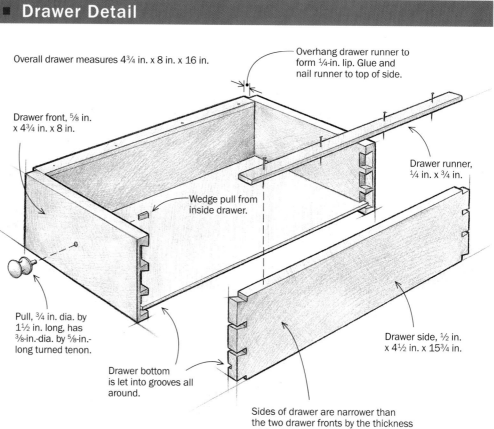

Overall drawer measures 4¾ in. x 8 in. x 16 in.

Overhang drawer runner to form ¼-in. lip. Glue and nail runner to top of side.

Drawer front, ⅝ in. x 4¾ in. x 8 in.

Drawer runner, ¼ in. x ¾ in.

Wedge pull from inside drawer.

Pull, ¾ in. dia. by 1½ in. long, has ⅜-in.-dia. by ⅝-in.-long turned tenon.

Drawer bottom is let into grooves all around.

Drawer side, ½ in. x 4½ in. x 15¾ in.

Sides of drawer are narrower than the two drawer fronts by the thickness of the drawer runner.

STANDS CHANGE ALONG WITH SHAKERS

The sewing stand gracefully expresses the Shaker principles of economy, utility and order. Economy is reflected in the small amount of wood needed to make one. Utility and order are evident if you consider that the stands were used for sewing and other occupations of Shaker community sisters. The stands can be moved easily, and those with two drawers can accommodate two sewers.

There were several versions of the Shaker sewing stand (see the bottom photo). The differences are mostly due to regional and cultural influences. Knowing a bit of Shaker furniture history helps explain how the differences came to be.

FURNITURE STYLES DRIVEN BY RELIGION AND WORK ETHICS

Shaker furniture passed through three somewhat distinct stylistic periods. The first is the Primitive period (about 1790-1820). It is marked by furniture that usually is heavy and plain in form, crudely made, but strong and functional.

In the Classic period (about 1820 to 1860), the pieces show greater utility, simplicity and perfection—all attributable to spiritual inspiration, dedication to the Shaker community and skill. This was the golden age of Shaker furnituremaking.

Victorian Shaker pieces, the most recent, have more decoration, such as moldings, ornate turnings, contrasting woods and fancy, commercially made pulls. These ornate elements were used to lure new members after the Civil War.

VARIATIONS ON A STAND

The earliest sewing stands probably had one drawer. One of the oldest stands I measured had a pedestal with three peg legs at the bottom and a turned transitional element on top, just below the drawer case. Stands with a single drawer surrounded by a yoke likely came shortly thereafter. They may or may not have Queen Anne (serpentine-style) legs, like the one shown in preceding pages.

The most recent sewing stands often have two drawers suspended from the tabletop. Cleats on the upper sides of the drawers slide in hangers. The hangers, attached to the table's underside, help retain flatness in the top. Many of these later stands had three Sheraton-style legs that give an umbrella shape to the base (see the photo at left). These two-drawer sewing stands are especially popular in America and are eagerly sought by antique-furniture collectors. Like most single-drawer stands, the two-drawer variety can be opened from the back.

AMERICA'S SHAKER ERA. Robert Treanor reproduced the tables above (from left): an early peg-leg stand, a Classic-period stand and a two-drawer stand (original shown at top), the most modern of the three.

CHRIS BECKSVOORT

Build a Shaker Round Stand

Having built almost 70 round stands, I still continue to revise and refine the shape and dimensions in an effort to achieve the perfect shape. The Shakers built a variety of round stands. They were conveniently placed near reading chairs, desks, worktables, benches and beds because the Shakers did all after-dark work by candlelight. That's why round stands are often called candle stands. Although crude at first, the designs became more refined and delicate during the early 19th century.

The pinnacle of round-stand design was achieved by a Shaker craftsman from Hancock, Mass., in the first half of the 1800s. The original stand is now in New York's Metropolitan Museum of Art. The stand consists of a ½-in.-thick by 18-in.-dia. top with a rounded edge, and the stand's tabletop is attached to the post by a cross brace. The post is a 3-in.-dia. turning resembling a wine bottle, with a ⅛-in. indentation at the bottom to accept the legs. The post is topped with a tulip swelling that has a round tenon to fit into the cross brace. The legs are a smooth cyma curve flowing out of the post with an arched curve below. The shape of the post is reflected in the profile of the cyma curve, and the thickness of the leg tapers from ¾ in. at the intersection with the post, to ½ in. at the tip. Overall, it is a design so clean, so simple, it cannot be improved upon.

As far as I know, there are no measured drawings of this round stand, although pictures and overall dimensions appear in several books. The measured drawing shown on p. 57 is by no means definitive, but it is as close as I have been able to come without actually measuring the original.

TURNING THE POST

Like the original, I made this round stand out of clear black cherry. I turned the post into a 3-in.-dia. cylinder on the lathe, and then I laid out detail lines, as shown in the drawing.

Although the turning is fairly straightforward, there are several locations where tolerances are critical. The first is the tenon diameter. I turned the tenon slightly oversized with a parting tool. Then I drilled a hole into a piece of scrap to test the diameter of the tenon. This way, I could turn the diameter for a perfect match to the drill bit I used to drill the cross brace.

Next I sized the neck just below the tulip, using the parting tool and caliper. Then I roughed out the shaft, turned the tulip and undercut the shoulder of the tulip using the tip of a diamond-point tool. With the top of the post completed, I moved the tool rest to the other end and cut the reduced cylinder at the bottom. The actual dimension is not critical, but the cylinder must be perfectly straight to attach the legs properly. The best way to achieve that is with a straight, hardwood block wrapped in

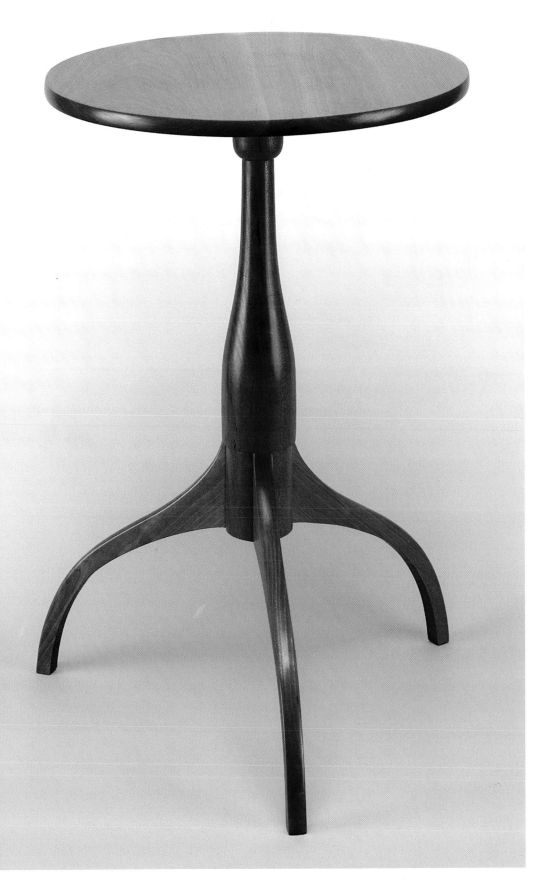

THE PINNACLE OF ROUND-STAND DESIGN is reflected in this table based on a piece built by a Shaker craftsman from Hancock, Mass., circa 1830. Whether as a side table, end table, night stand or reading lamp stand, the smooth, flowing lines of this stand will brighten any room.

sandpaper and used in conjunction with a dial caliper.

Shaping the main shaft is the last step and visually the most difficult. There are only two reference points to rely on, the 1¼ in. dia. at the top and 3 in. dia. at the bottom. A series of light cuts with a sharp gouge got me to the elongated cyma curve that I was after. Then I sanded progressively from 120-grit to 600-grit. Finally, I reversed the rotation of the lathe and then polished the post with #000 steel wool.

DOVETAILING THE POST

Cutting the dovetail slots for the legs was the next step. Ordinarily, I make one stand at a time and find it just as fast (and a lot more fun) to cut the dovetail slots with a

handsaw, chisel and mallet. But this time, I had two orders of two stands each, plus I needed a stand for display, so I decided to make a cradle to hold the post for cutting the slots with a dovetail bit mounted in my spindle mortiser. An interesting and perhaps more approachable alternative for the home shop is the neat, on-the-lathe, router technique shown in the story on p. 59.

MAKING THE LEGS

The legs were cut using the pattern shown in the drawing. By tracing the pattern on the stock, I could be sure that the grain ran from the upper corner of the leg to the lower end for the greatest possible strength. For consistency of color, all three legs were cut from the same board. After the legs were bandsawn, I stacked and taped them together with masking tape. Then I used a disc sander and a pneumatic sanding drum mounted on my lathe to clean up the shape, as shown in the photo at left, sanding one untaped side at a time.

To cut the dovetail pins on the legs (see the top photo on p. 58), I used the same ⅜-in.-dia. dovetail bit I used to cut the slots. Only this time, the bit was in a table-mounted router. I set the depth of cut to the same depth as the dovetailed slot and slid the fence over to cut a dovetail just thicker than the ⅜-in.-dia. bit. Then, through trial-and-error cuts on a piece of scrap, I adjusted the fence until the dovetail pin slid snugly into the slot in the post.

The leg thickness was tapered on the jointer. I set the jointer to ⅛-in. depth of cut and used a wide push stick with a notch to hold the end of the leg. I slowly and carefully placed the upper section of the leg on the outfeed table, as shown in the bottom photo on p. 58. Then I pushed the leg across the blade, turned it over and repeated the process on the reverse side.

After completing the other two legs, I beltsanded them to 150-grit and dry-fit them into the post. Using a sharp, pointed knife, I scribed the top of each leg where it joins the post. At the same time, I marked the bottom of the post at the lower edge of

SANDING ALL THE LEGS TO THE SAME SHAPE is easier if the blanks are taped together before sanding to the layout lines. Bandsawing the legs close to the line reduces sanding.

This drawing is the author's interpretation of an original Shaker round stand built in the first half of the 1800s at Hancock, Mass. The original is now in the Metropolitan Museum of Art in New York City.

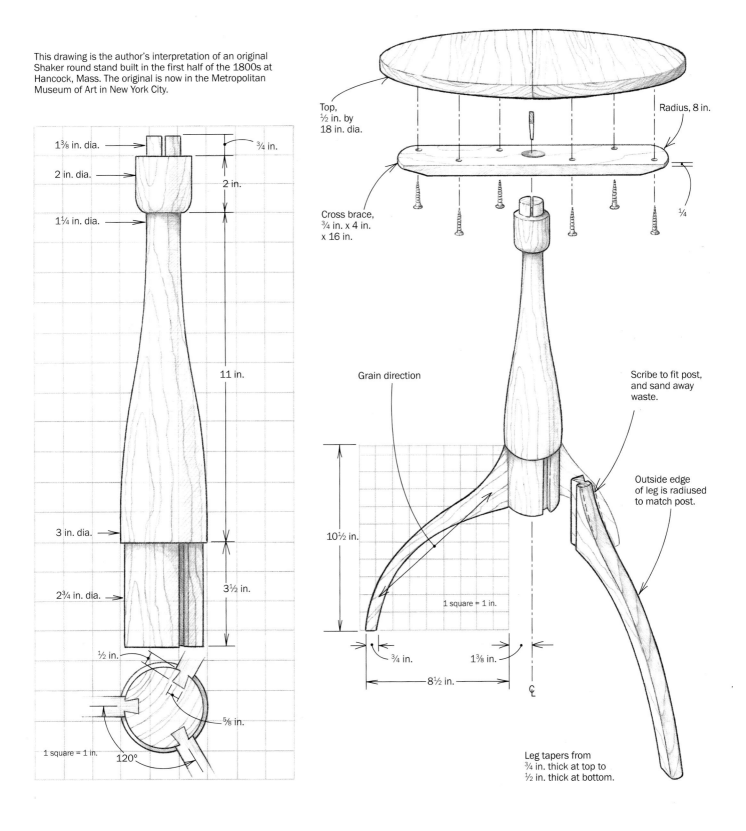

1³⁄₈ in. dia.

2 in. dia.

1¼ in. dia.

¾ in.

2 in.

11 in.

3 in. dia.

2¾ in. dia.

3½ in.

½ in.

⁵⁄₈ in.

1 square = 1 in.

120°

Top,
½ in. by
18 in. dia.

Radius, 8 in.

Cross brace,
¾ in. x 4 in.
x 16 in.

¼

Grain direction

Scribe to fit post,
and sand away
waste.

Outside edge
of leg is radiused
to match post.

10½ in.

¾ in.

1³⁄₈ in.

8½ in.

1 square = 1 in.

Leg tapers from
¾ in. thick at top to
½ in. thick at bottom.

SLIDING DOVETAIL PINS ARE CUT EASILY WITH A DOVETAIL BIT in a table-mounted router. The author tests the setup with scrap to be sure the pin fits snugly in the socket.

TAPERING THE LEG THICKNESS ON THE JOINTER requires carefully placing the pin end of the leg on the outfeed table and making a single ⅛-in.-deep pass on each side.

the leg. I removed the legs and bandsawed the post to length. Then I sanded the legs to the scribed mark on the pneumatic sanding drum. The top of the legs have the same radius as the post and blended smoothly into the post when reassembled. All legs were then sanded to 600-grit and glued into place.

COMPLETING THE TOP AND CROSS BRACE

I glued up the top from two pieces cut from a single 10-in.-wide board to match color and grain. While the top was drying, I cut the cross brace, rounded the ends and drilled the center hole for the post tenon. Then I tapered the rounded ends back about 2 in. so that only ¼ in. of thickness was left on the ends. Finally, I sanded the brace from 120-grit to 600-grit.

I dry-fit the brace to the tenon, making sure it was perpendicular to one leg. I considered this leg the front of the table and picked the one on the quartersawn side of the post. I made a mark across the tenon, perpendicular to the grain of the brace. With a handsaw, I cut a slot in the tenon and made a wedge to fit. Then I applied glue to the hole in the brace, slid the brace into position and hammered in the wedge. The post must be hand-held, or the base of the post must be supported on the corner of the bench because the legs won't stand up to these direct hammer blows.

After the tenon was trimmed, I put the base aside to dry while I cut and sanded the top. I bandsawed the top just shy of the layout line and disc sanded to the line. I radiused the top's edge on a slightly deflated pneumatic-drum sander. This could also be done by hand. Although a router would make quick work of shaping the edge, I've never found an appropriate bit with the subtle radius I prefer. I then sanded the edge and both sides of the top to 600-grit.

Before attaching the top, I sanded the bottom of the post flush with the bottom edge of the legs. I lightly chamfered the foot at the bottom of the legs, so they don't splinter and catch on carpeting.

I screwed on the top, centered on the cross brace and oriented with the brace perpendicular to the grain of the top. The screw holes near the outside edge were elongated to allow for cross-grain movement of the top. The stand was now ready for finishing. The original has a clear varnish finish, but I've used a rubbed oil finish on mine.

ROBERT TREANOR

ROUTER MAKES QUICK WORK OF SLIDING DOVETAILS

As a teacher, I often suggest a round stand as a first project for beginning students. The stand's small scale and frugal use of material make it approachable, and the level of complexity in several processes, including hand-cutting the sliding dovetails, make it a nearly perfect project for the novice. Also, the students always appreciate the attractive piece of furniture they walk away with.

As one who believes teaching by example is sound, I, too, would cut the joints by hand. That is until I was faced with having to make three stands in short order. To speed up production, I developed a lathe-mounted jig (see the photo at right) that let me cut accurate and repeatable dovetail sockets with a router.

CONSTRUCTING THE JIG

I constructed the jig with medium density fiberboard (MDF) because of its stability and flatness. Other materials may be used; however, avoid solid stock because of its propensity to move. It is vital that the jig's pieces be square and accurate so that the router riding on top of the jig cuts parallel to the centerline of the lathe.

I began by cutting two pieces of MDF for the sides of the jig. The height of the jig needs to be equal to the swing of your lathe and at least one-half the diameter of the spindle you are turning. The length is limited by the length of the project mounted in the lathe. I cut a dado for the bottom of the jig about 1 in. up from the lower edge of the side. The width of the bottom depends on the width of your lathe bed. On the underside of the bottom, I milled a shallow dado equal in width to the gap in the lathe bed. Into this dado, I fit another block of MDF that acts as a key to permit

CUTTING SLIDING DOVETAIL SOCKETS IS A SIMPLE TASK WITH THIS LATHE-MOUNTED JIG. The jig must be square, accurate and parallel to the axis of the lathe for proper attachment of the legs. The stability of medium-density fiberboard makes it a good choice for jigs.

the assembled jig to slide along the bed of the lathe in line with the axis of the lathe centers.

I glued and screwed the jig together, checking carefully to be sure the sides were square to the bottom. Once positioned, I added a few braces to hold the sides square. After the glue dried, I drilled a hole through the bottom of the jig for the bolt that clamps the jig to the lathe bed.

USING THE JIG

To use the jig, I unplugged the lathe and clamped the jig to the lathe bed. My lathe has an indexing headstock, so I can lock the turning in position. If your lathe doesn't have a built-in indexing system, it's fairly easy to add a shop-built indexing wheel to the headstock.

I positioned the router so its bit would be at top dead center of the turning, and I adjusted the router's edge guide to ride along the side of the jig to control the cut. I chucked a straight bit in the router and then cut flats on the turning where the legs will butt against the post. The width of the flat needs to be just a hair wider than the thickness of the leg. After cutting

the first flat, I rotated the turning 120°, repeated the process for the second flat and again for the third flat.

With the flats cut, I wasted away the bulk of the joint in two or three passes with a ½-in.-dia. straight bit, indexing the head as before. I completed the socket by switching to a dovetail bit and routing the sloping, dovetailed sides of the joint in one pass, as shown in the photo below.

TO CUT THE DOVETAIL SOCKETS, the router rides on top of the jig, with an edge guide positioned to center the bit on the table post. The author first hogs out most of the socket waste with a straight bit and finally cuts the socket in one pass with a dovetail bit.

Projects &Techniques

GARRETT HACK

Building a Strong, Light Carcase

SIMPLE LINES, REMARKABLE WOODS AND STRUCTURAL INTEGRITY combine with impeccable craftsmanship to make the author's Shaker-inspired hall table a jewel in wood. All drawer faces are from one pear board; the carcase is carefully grain- and figure-matched bird's-eye maple, and the pulls and pegs are rosewood.

Some people think that the larger a piece is, the more difficult it is to build. That's true to a certain extent, but designing and building smaller, more delicate pieces that still will stand up to the rigors of normal household life—kids and dogs included—is a challenge of its own. Perhaps the most difficult situation is the table or desk with drawers.

Three pieces of wood joined to form a U-shape have virtually no structural integrity. Exert a little pressure on one side, and the corner joint will fail. In contrast, if you join four pieces of wood to form a box, you've got a fairly sturdy structure. Put a top (or bottom) on the box, and you have a structure that will take some abuse. But if you cut a bunch of holes in the front of the piece (drawer openings), you've eliminated much of its strength.

Furnituremakers have come up with various ways of strengthening desks and tables whose fronts are mostly drawers, such as beefing up the frame internally and using heavy-duty front rails. Neither of these is ideal. An internal frame (basically, a shallow box around the internal perimeter of the carcase, sometimes with a crossbar) reduces useable drawer space, and thick, bulky front rails may fit the bill structurally, but they aren't the most aesthetic solution. My solution addresses both of these shortcomings.

Unless you use it to stand on while changing a light bulb, most of the stress on a piece of furniture like this is from rack-ing, not downward compression. What's needed then are not massive front rails, but deep rails—rails that tie the front of the piece to the three solid sides of the carcase and provide maximum resistance to racking. Together with the table's leg-and-apron construction, these thin, deep rails ensure a piece of furniture that is tough but still looks quite refined, as shown in the photo on the facing page.

CARCASE JOINERY

After I've prepared all my stock and turned the legs for this side table, I begin cutting the joinery. I used a pair of haunched tenons for each leg-to-apron joint (see the drawing on p. 63). Adding a haunch to a tenon increases the glue area of the joint, making it stronger. Even more importantly, though, the haunches increase the mechanical resistance of the joint to twisting.

I lay out my mortises first, clamping all the legs together side by side so that the mortises are all positioned identically. I make all of the mortises with a shop-built slot mortiser, but if you don't have a mortiser, a plunge router and mortising jig (or mortise chisel and mallet) will also work fine. Next I square the ends and then chop the haunch mortises with a sharp paring chisel. To keep the haunch mortises consistent, one to another, I make a small pattern from scrap, and use the pattern as a depth and angle check.

ROSEWOOD PEGS STRENGTHEN THE JOINT, and they add a distinctive touch to the author's table. The adjustable wrench keeps the pegs properly oriented, parallel to the case's top and sides.

After I've cut all the leg mortises and the corresponding apron tenons, I cut, plane and scrape the front rails. It's important that the faces of the rails that accept the stiles be finish-planed now so that you don't alter the fit by removing stock after cutting the joinery. I also cut the bead into the lower front rail and aprons now, using a scratch stock. I clamp the three front rails together edge to edge to align them, as I did the legs, and I mark out the tenons at each end and the dovetailed slots for the stiles.

I rout the dovetailed slots first, and then work out the pin width and depth on one end of each of the stiles, leaving them long so I can rout a few trial pins. Then, once I have a good pin, I cut the stiles to length and rout the remaining pins. Next I mortise the front legs for the rails, mortise the rails themselves for the drawer runner and kicker tenons and then cut the front rail tenons (see the drawing on p. 63 for joinery details).

Because I wanted maximum joint strength, I mitered the apron tenons at each rear leg. Mitering the tenons allows me to make them longer than would be possible if their ends were square, increasing the glue surface and strengthening the joint. I mark the cutoff line on the tenon by sticking a sharply tapered pencil in through the opposite mortise.

While the leg-to-apron joints are still together, I also score the legs where the tops of the aprons intersect them and carry these marks around each leg with a sharp knife. I crosscut the legs just shy of this mark. Then I plane the legs level with the rest of the carcase after glue-up so that legs and aprons are all precisely even.

I drill the pocket holes in the aprons, using an angled fixture on my drill press to hold the apron in place. I use a Forstner bit first to provide a flat seat for the screw head and then follow with a slightly over-sized twist bit to allow for seasonal movement of the wood. I generally prefer buttons for attaching tabletops, but for this small a table, either the buttons would have to be so thin that they would have broken, or they would have to be so thick that they would have interfered with the drawers.

ASSEMBLY

After I finish planing and scraping all parts not already smoothed, I begin the assembly: first both rear legs and apron and then the two front legs and two bottom drawer rails. After the glue has set on these first two subassemblies, I join them with the side aprons.

The top drawer rail finishes the case assembly (see the drawing). This rail was sometimes left out by the Shakers in similar pieces, but it's an important element when trying to maximize strength while retaining a delicate-looking carcase. Not only does it add strength to the carcase but also it completes the drawer face frame visually and drops the top drawers slightly so that they're more accessible beneath the overhang.

I cut the dovetailed ends of the rail first, lay it in position, scribe around it and chop the mortise to receive it. Then I drill and countersink a few holes in the rail to secure the top and glue and screw (insurance) the rail into place. I level the top of the case with a jointer plane, working slowly around the piece to take care not to tear out any fibers as I pass over the legs. I finish the carcase assembly by tapping the stiles home into the stopped sliding dovetail slots in the

Shaker Side Table

Note: Measurements do not include tenon or dovetail lengths.

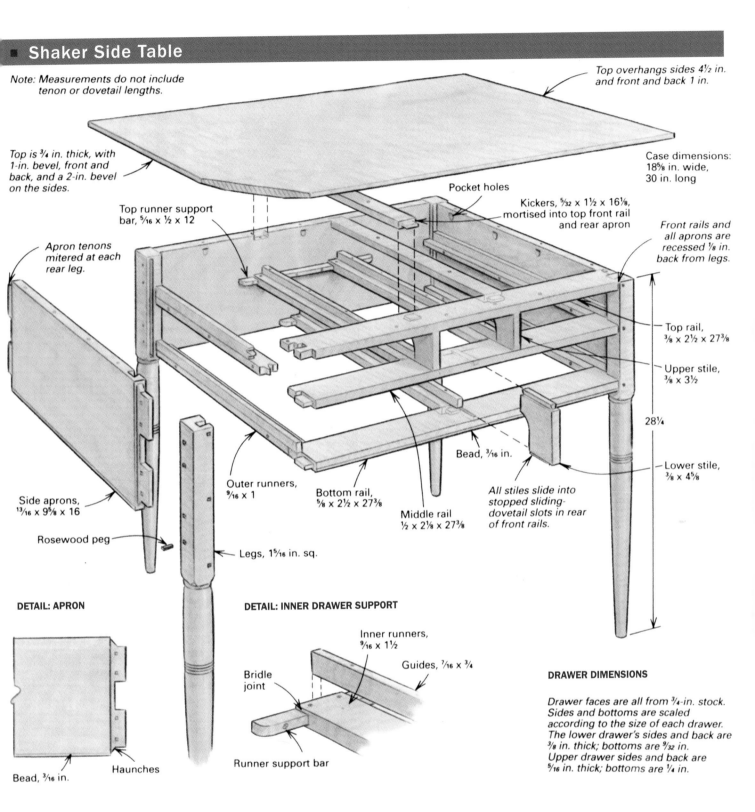

Top overhangs sides 4½ in. and front and back 1 in.

Top is ¾ in. thick, with 1-in. bevel, front and back, and a 2-in. bevel on the sides.

Case dimensions: 18⅝ in. wide, 30 in. long

Pocket holes

Kickers, ⁵⁄₃₂ x 1½ x 16⅛, mortised into top front rail and rear apron

Top runner support bar, ⁵⁄₁₆ x ½ x 12

Front rails and all aprons are recessed ⅛ in. back from legs.

Apron tenons mitered at each rear leg.

Top rail, ⅜ x 2½ x 27⅜

Upper stile, ⅜ x 3½

28¼

Side aprons, ¹³⁄₁₆ x 9⅝ x 16

Rosewood peg

Outer runners, ⁹⁄₁₆ x 1

Bottom rail, ⅝ x 2½ x 27⅜

Middle rail, ½ x 2⅛ x 27⅜

Bead, ³⁄₁₆ in.

All stiles slide into stopped sliding-dovetail slots in rear of front rails.

Lower stile, ⅜ x 4⅝

Legs, 1⁵⁄₁₆ in. sq.

DETAIL: APRON

Bead, ³⁄₁₆ in.

Haunches

DETAIL: INNER DRAWER SUPPORT

Inner runners, ⁹⁄₁₆ x 1½

Guides, ⁷⁄₁₆ x ¾

Bridle joint

Runner support bar

DRAWER DIMENSIONS

Drawer faces are all from ¾-in. stock. Sides and bottoms are scaled according to the size of each drawer. The lower drawer's sides and back are ⅜ in. thick; bottoms are ⁹⁄₃₂ in. Upper drawer sides and back are ⁵⁄₁₆ in. thick; bottoms are ¼ in.

front rails, dabbing just a bit of glue into the slots.

I pin all the joints with small, square rosewood pegs because they add mechanical strength to the joints and because I like the contrast with the maple. I mark out peg locations with an awl, rub a small square of masking tape over the hole-to-be (it prevents tearout when drilling) and drill my holes. To make it easier to fit the pegs into their holes, I square the top third of each hole roughly with a paring chisel, pare the bottom two-thirds of each peg fairly round and taper the end of each peg with a little pencil sharpener. I drive the pegs home with a 12-oz. hammer (rosewood is very dense and not likely to be damaged by the metal). When hammering, I hold onto the pegs with a small adjustable wrench to keep the pegs parallel to top and sides (see the photo on p. 62). I tap the pegs home and then pare them almost flush with a chisel, finishing up with a block plane and a scraper.

The next step is to install the web frame: drawer runners, guides and kickers. If you want the drawers to glide smoothly, you must plane all wear surfaces glassy smooth (wax applied later will further reduce friction). The guides should be parallel to the carcase sides and the runners flush with the top of the drawer rails. I cut the guides so they're just shy of the stile faces and the rear of the carcase; that way, I only have to worry about the fit of the runners.

The runners for the top bay of drawers serve as kickers for the bottom drawers, preventing them from dropping down when they're partially open (see the drawing for details). I thickness the runner stock so that it's ⅛ in. thinner than the front rails, which allows the drawer to drop slightly but not scrape the kicker on opening. I thickness the top drawer kickers similarly.

I glue and screw the outside runners and guides into place. For the interior runners, I tenon the front end to slip into the mortises in the face-frame rails, and then I use a bridle joint at the rear to attach the runners to the support bars, as shown in the drawing above. The beauty of using this bridle joint is that it allows adjustment of the runners horizontally and vertically before

screwing the bar in, and it lets me install the runners and guides after the case is assembled, making that job considerably simpler.

I center the guides on the runners, apply glue and screw through the runners into the guides from below. Winding sticks help me get everything on the same plane, and a few sticks cut to exactly the widths of the drawer openings keep the guides parallel. The last parts to go in are the top drawer kickers, which I tenon into the top drawer rail at the front and set into a mortise at the top of the apron in the back. In addition to keeping the drawers from dropping when they're opened, the kickers also add to the overall integrity of the carcase.

I like to have the top and case completed and assembled before starting on drawers in case there's any tension between the carcase and top. I don't want any surprises (drawers binding, for example) after I've fitted the drawers (see the box on the facing page for how I build and fit drawers). I milled the boards for the top nearly to final thickness, matched and glued them and then finish-planed and scraped top and bottom.

I beveled the underside of the top all around, rough-cutting the bevel on the tablesaw and then finishing up with a sharp plane held askew. I drew a pencil line all around the edge as a guide for the bevel. This thin beveled edge is pleasant visually, lightening the top in appearance, but without diminishing the mass and the strength of the top in the middle. Before securing the top, I apply a coat of finish to both the top and bottom.

The finish is built up of thin coats of spar varnish, linseed oil and turpentine. I rub each coat in well, let it dry until it just starts to tack up and then vigorously rub off any excess. To bring out the contrasting grain of the bird's eyes, I add a small amount of Minwax Golden Oak oil stain to the varnish mixture. After three or four coats of this finish, inside and out, I polish the whole piece with steel wool and a mixture of beeswax, linseed oil and turpentine. I give the drawer runners, guides and bearing surfaces of the drawer sides the same treatment.

The trick to getting drawers to fit sweetly is to cut the faces to fit the openings exactly (see the bottom photo). If you can't fit a drawer in its opening, you can always plane the sides to fit—but you can't add any wood back if you start with a sloppy fit.

I cut and pare the dovetail pins on the drawer face first. Then I finish-plane the inside and outside of the drawer faces so that they are at final thickness before I mark and cut the tails at the front of the drawer sides. I also drill the holes for the tenon on the pull now.

To keep the drawers both strong and light, I varied the drawer side thickness, so the smaller upper drawers have thinner sides than those below. As with the drawer faces, I finish-plane the insides and outsides of the drawer sides before marking out the tails, except for the first few inches of the outside face around the joint. I leave this area unplaned at this stage because I'll be cleaning up the joint with my plane after glue-up anyway.

Once I've cut and test-fitted the drawer-face dovetails, I cut the sides to length and rout sliding dovetail slots from the bottom of the sides about ¾ in. in from the end. Because the thickness of the drawer back won't affect the fit of the sliding dovetail joint, I finish-plane the backs after I

have fit the joint. I used the tablesaw to plow drawer bottom grooves into the faces and sides. I also set aside a piece of scrap with the groove in it to use later for sizing the beveled drawer bottoms.

Beginning with the face dovetails, I assemble each drawer, squaring each corner as I tap it home and clamping the joint if necessary to keep it square. Often I won't even use clamps, though, because a properly fitting set of dovetails doesn't require clamping. After I've joined the drawer face and sides, I slide the back into its dovetailed slot in the side. When the back is two-thirds home, I put a small amount of glue in the slot and on the pin and finish tapping it home. Then I check (and adjust, if necessary) again for square by measuring the diagonals and comparing. I set the drawer on my tablesaw's flat-ground top while the glue is setting up. This way, twist won't be built into the drawer from sitting on a less than flat surface.

I proportioned the thickness of the drawer bottom to the drawer sides by eye and by feel: thinner bottoms for the smaller upper drawers and thicker bottoms for the larger drawers below. I beveled the underside of the drawer bottoms, so I could keep the bottom thicker in the middle (and therefore stronger). And I could position the bottom a little deeper in the drawer and still have enough lip to support the bottom

PLANING DRAWER SIDES TO FIT is a painstaking process. Hack takes a few passes with a plane and checks the drawer in its opening. The chamois between the drawer side and the board supporting it protects the inside face of the drawer side.

securely. Also, a beveled bottom has a certain elegance. I glue up the bottoms from thicknessed stock, rip and crosscut each bottom to size, finish-plane the top surface and then rough out the bevels on the tablesaw. Then I plane each bevel until it fits in the grooved piece of scrap I saved for testing this fit, finish-plane the underside of the bottom and slide it home into the drawer frame, securing it with two screws at one-third points across the bottom into the drawer back.

The first step in fitting drawers is to plane the area I left unplaned around the half-blind dovetails joining the drawer faces to the sides. Then I just plane both sides equally, constantly testing the drawer in the opening until there is a total of about ¹⁄₁₆-in. play from side to side, as shown in the bottom photo. (For larger drawers, I'd leave a bit more clearance.)

Next I level the bottom of the sides and face with a jointer plane, working with the grain all the way around. I also ease all the edges, so they're more pleasing visually and tactilely and to help the drawers glide more smoothly. Once the bottom is level, I flip the drawer over and level the top, stopping often to check the drawer's fit. For drawers of this size, ¹⁄₁₆-in. play at the top is plenty for seasonal movement.

DRAWER FACE BLANKS THAT ARE SNUG BUT DO NOT BIND are key to sweetly fitting drawers. Hack leaves the drawers snug at this point, so there will be a minimum amount of play when he planes the sides.

CHRIS BECKSVOORT

Build a Bookcase
with Doors

The essence of good design is a piece of furniture that seems right just the way it is. There should be nothing to add and nothing to take away to improve it. That's what I aimed for with this cherry bookcase. It was to be Shaker inspired, quiet and unpretentious, but not boring.

The bookcase needed to fit beneath a window sill, so it is relatively small, about 24 in. wide and 40 in. high. Its appearance and size are not overpowering, so I relied on careful workmanship and just a few details to carry the design. Each of these construction details—a dovetailed molding at the top of the case, a mitered base and a strip of wood whose end grain doesn't show just above the doors—required a fair amount of extra work. The details don't jump out at you, but together they give the bookcase an appeal that it wouldn't otherwise have.

DOVETAILS HOLD THE CASE TOGETHER

The basic structure of this bookcase is quite simple: Two sides dovetailed to the top and three shelves connected to the sides with sliding dovetails. A frame-and-panel back is set into a rabbet at the case's back. To begin, I milled, crosscut and ripped to width the top and two sides from a single wide cherry board. I cut the rabbet for the back panel in the rear inside edge of each piece, and then I laid out and cut the dovetailed slots in the top. Because the top overhangs the sides by ¾ in. at the front of the case, the half-slot there is set back ¾ in. from the edge. To lay out the pins on the top of the sides, I used a picture-frame clamp, which holds the top and a side at precisely 90° to each other (see the photo at left on p. 68). Then I cut and chopped the pins.

I cut the foot profiles in the sides on the bandsaw, then laid out and routed the dovetailed slots for the three fixed shelves using a shop-built fixture to guide the router. Before gluing the top and sides together, I sanded the insides. To be sure the top and sides glued up square, I placed a spacer stick between the two front feet when gluing and clamping the three pieces together (see the center photo on p. 68).

Routing the sliding dovetails on the ends of the shelves was next. After planing the shelves to thickness, then ripping and crosscutting them, I used the offcuts to set the fence on my router table. Once I had a perfect fit, I routed the dovetails on both ends of all three shelves and sanded them.

One at a time, I slid each shelf into its slot from the front, stopping when 3 in. of shelf was still exposed. At this point, I applied glue to the dovetails at the top and to the slots underneath and tapped the shelf home, stopping when it was flush with the back rabbet and with the front (see the right photo on p. 68). I clamped the case from side to side, both front and back.

I built the frame-and-panel back about ⅛ in. wider and longer than its opening. To fit it to the case, I started by running the top edge over the jointer, fitting one side and then, carefully, the other. I was careful to take even amounts off both sides. With help from a little block plane, the back eased in nicely.

After sanding the back, I held it in place, marked the location of the shelves on the back of the frame and glued the back into its rabbet. After the glue had dried, I drilled holes for 6d finishing nails at the marks I had made, one at the center of each shelf and one near each end. I countersunk these nails about ⅛ in. deep and plugged the holes with whittled down cherry pegs. Then I sanded the back and softened all the edges with a worn piece of 220-grit paper.

There's only about 1 in. of case side extending below the bottom shelf and only the first and last 3 in. of the shelf is glued. So I glued and screwed two small blocks on the underside of the bottom shelf, one at the center of each end. I sanded the bottom edges of the sides and back, as well as the angled sides of the feet. A belt sander quickly removed the rough spots, and a little hand-sanding eliminated the scratches.

Miters Solve Two Aesthetic Problems

I planned to hang the double doors so they went all the way to the outside edges of the case rather than inside the case. This would leave the doors standing ¾ in. off the front of the bookcase unless I added two horizontal strips of wood across the case front to even things out. One strip would go just above the doors and one just below. But I didn't want end grain showing on the sides of the case at the ends of the top strip, and I wasn't sure how to integrate the bottom strip into the foot assembly without it looking awkward. As it turned out, the solutions to both these design problems involved miters.

For the top strip, I decided to miter both ends and glue on little blocks oriented in the same direction as the case sides. Because the strip was glued to the overhang of the top as well as to the edge of the case sides,

the end grain glue-up wasn't a problem. I started by cutting a strip ¹³⁄₁₆ in. sq. and 28 in. long from heartwood scrap left over from the sides. I set the blade at 45° and ripped just shy of 4 in. into this strip on the tablesaw, keeping the kerf on the waste side of the diagonal center and carefully backing out the strip from the blade. I crosscut the strip at 24 in. and set that piece aside for a moment. Then I cut two ⅞-in.-long pieces from the ripped triangular section. I mitered one end of the 24-in.-long piece at 45°, held it in place on the case, then marked and mitered the other end. I glued one of the little ⅞-in.-long blocks at each end of the 24-in.-long piece, using masking tape as a clamp.

After the glue had dried, I carefully jointed the strip at the ends and ripped it to ⁷⁄₁₆ in. wide by ¼ in. deep. I glued the piece to the top of the case, under the overhang. As a result, all you can see from the front or sides is face grain.

■ Tips for smoother dovetailing

Picture-frame clamp keeps top and side at 90° for layout.

KEEP THE CASE SQUARE. A piece of scrap cut to the interior dimension of the bookcase and placed at its base keeps the sides of the bookcase parallel and ensures that the top will clamp up square to the sides.

SLIDING DOVETAILS ARE GLUED JUST AT THE ENDS. By leaving the joint dry until it's within 2 in. or 3 in. of home, the author prevents the dovetails from binding. The mechanical connection is plenty strong even without glue in the middle.

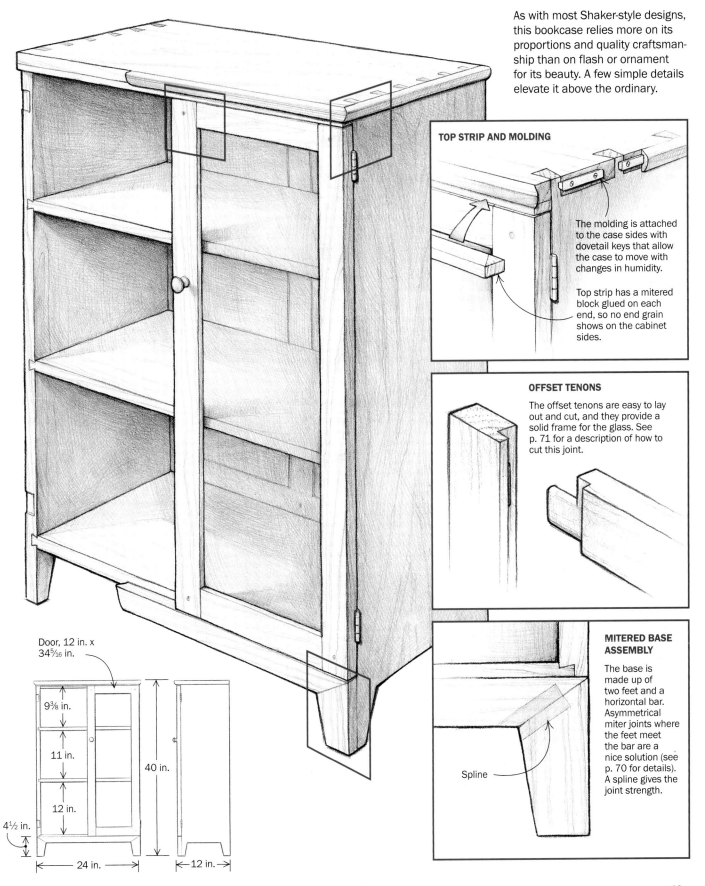

As with most Shaker-style designs, this bookcase relies more on its proportions and quality craftsmanship than on flash or ornament for its beauty. A few simple details elevate it above the ordinary.

TOP STRIP AND MOLDING

The molding is attached to the case sides with dovetail keys that allow the case to move with changes in humidity.

Top strip has a mitered block glued on each end, so no end grain shows on the cabinet sides.

OFFSET TENONS

The offset tenons are easy to lay out and cut, and they provide a solid frame for the glass. See p. 71 for a description of how to cut this joint.

MITERED BASE ASSEMBLY

The base is made up of two feet and a horizontal bar. Asymmetrical miter joints where the feet meet the bar are a nice solution (see p. 70 for details). A spline gives the joint strength.

Spline

Door, 12 in. x 34⁵⁄₁₆ in.

9³⁄₈ in.

11 in.

12 in.

40 in.

4¹⁄₂ in.

24 in.

12 in.

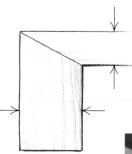

1. Lay out the miter. Holding the horizontal bar on the foot piece, the author marks the face of the foot and the bottom edge of the horizontal bar.

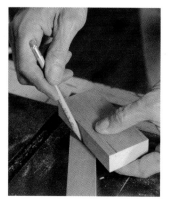

2. Connect the dots. Straight lines between these marks and the corner of each piece establish the miters.

3. Cut to the line. The author uses a bandsaw to cut each miter, then trues them up on a disc sander. A handsaw and plane would work just as well.

4. Attach the base assembly to the case by gluing it to the case sides and the bottom half of the bottom shelf. The top half of the bottom shelf is exposed and acts as a doorstop.

The foot assembly—two feet and a horizontal bar connecting them—is made using asymmetrical miters (see the drawing and photos on the facing page). I started with a single piece ¾ in. thick, 2 in. wide and 34 in. long. Then I cut a 5-in.-long piece off each end. After ripping the long piece to 1¼ in. wide, I laid out the miters, as shown in photos 1 and 2 on the facing page. I cut the miters close to the line on the bandsaw (see photo 3 on the facing page) and sanded right up to the line on a disc sander.

To give this joint some strength (it's just end grain meeting end grain), I used a ¼-in.-thick spline that stops short of the top of the joint, so it's hidden from view (see the drawing of the mitered base assembly on p. 69). When I glued up the assembly, I used a bar clamp to pull the joint in from end to end and two hand screws to exert pressure top to bottom. Once the glue had dried, I ran the whole assembly along the rip fence, crosscutting the legs to 4½ in. Then I cut the foot angles and trimmed the protruding splines on the bandsaw. I sanded the underside of the horizontal bar and the foot angles next and glued the assembly onto the case (see photo 4 on the facing page).

To make the feet a little beefier, I installed glue blocks on their inside corners where the sides meet the front and the back. I took a piece about ⅞-in.-sq. and 10 in. long and ripped it diagonally on the bandsaw, using a V-block as a cradle. Then I held a piece in each corner, marked and cut it to its actual length and planed the bandsawn face smooth. I glued one into each corner, using a spring clamp for pressure.

After beltsanding the feet flush on the bottom, I drilled a ⅛-in.-deep, ¾-in.-dia. hole in the center of the bottom of each foot with a Forstner bit. I drilled a 1⁄16-in.-dia. pilot hole in the center of each of those holes, then nailed in nylon furniture glides. Only about 1⁄16 in. protrudes, so they are not visible unless you happen to be lying on the floor. After using a block plane to chamfer the feet lightly all the way around, I sanded the whole case to 320-grit. Then I followed up with 0000 steel wool and eased any sharp edges.

FRAME JOINERY THAT YOU DON'T HAVE TO MEASURE

The offset tenon shoulders on the rails make these door-frame joints look more difficult than they really are. The only real trick to getting joints that fit perfectly is to use the first shoulder as a reference when laying out the second, as shown below.

Rabbet and mortise the stile first. Start by cutting rabbets in rails and stiles and routing or chopping out mortises in stiles.

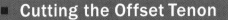
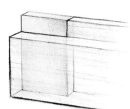

1. First shoulder. Cut outside shoulder of tenon. Determine depth by the rabbet; length is equal to the depth of the mortise plus the rabbet.

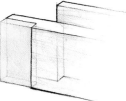

2. Scribe, don't measure. Rest the shoulder of the rail on the inside edge of the stile, then mark the location of the second shoulder.

3. Cut second shoulder. The inside shoulder of the tenon is shorter to compensate for the rabbet in the stile.

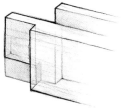

4. Size the tenon. The tenon should be slightly smaller than the mortise.

5. Round the tenon. Use a knife or a chisel to ease the tenon corners and to get them to fit the rounded mortise.

My 10¢ trick for hanging doors

HINGE LOCATION IS MARKED ON THE EDGE OF THE CASE SIDES.
Pinching a dime—about ¾₄ in. thick—between the top of the stile and the case gives the author the reveal he wants at the top of the door.
Waste is removed with a laminate trimmer; then the joint is cleaned up with a paring chisel.

DOOR-FRAME JOINERY LOOKS TRICKY—BUT ISN'T

The two door frames for this bookcase are joined with mortise-and-tenon joints and are rabbeted in the back to accept glass. I used quartersawn stock for the frames, both to minimize wood movement and for appearance. After choosing the frame pieces and cutting them to length, I rabbeted them, making two cuts on the tablesaw. I saved the waste strips from the rabbeting operation for use as glass retaining bars. I

laid out and bored the mortises in the four stiles next.

The rail tenons are a bit complex conceptually because they have offset shoulders, but the work is actually quite simple. The drawings at left explain the process. I cut the tenons on the tablesaw, setting the fence for the shoulder distance and using the miter gauge to keep the cut straight. Then I eliminated the waste up to the cheek by running the rails back and forth over the blade beginning at its leading edge, taking off just a little with each pass over the blade. As the drawing at left shows, the trick to getting the shoulders to line up perfectly is to mark the second shoulder while using the first as a depth stop.

After all the tenons were cut, I rounded over their edges with a knife. Once they all fit, I glued and clamped the frames together, checking to be sure they were square. When the glue had dried, I pinned the joints all the way through with ¼-in.-dia., ⅞-in.-long sections of cherry dowel. I used only one pin per joint because the tenons are quite small. Then I sanded and steel-wooled the doors as I had the case.

Fitting the doors was straightforward. I placed the case on its back on sawhorses and aligned the first door flush with the outside edge. I marked and jointed the top square, then the bottom, and repeated the process for the other door. I always try to get a reveal of ⅟₁₆ in. or less at the top and about ³⁄₃₂ in. at the bottom. Doors droop over time; they never creep up. Finally, I planed the inside edges of the two doors to get a ³⁄₃₂-in. reveal between them. Because I used quartersawn stock, total movement for both doors, side to side, should be less than ⅟₁₆ in.

I hinged the doors with 1½-in. broad brass hinges from Whitechapel Ltd. (P.O. Box 11719, Jackson, WY 83002; 800-468-5534). I laid out the hinges in the doors first, scribing around the hinges with a knife. I routed out most of the waste for the door-hinge mortises using a laminate trimmer, and then I cleaned up the corners and edges with a wide chisel. I installed the hinges in the doors, waxing the screws to ease their entry.

To lay out the positions of the hinge mortises on the edges of the case sides, I laid the doors on the case, one at a time.

I made sure the outside edge was flush while I pinched a dime between the top rail and the top of the case (see the inset photo on the facing page). I made a knife mark on both sides of each hinge, then removed the doors.

To lay out the perimeter of these hinge mortises, I laid a door upside down on a sawhorse, right next to the case, and held a hinge in place between the knife marks I'd

just made. The barrel of the hinge acted as a depth stop, allowing me to mark out the perimeter of the mortise.

Before attaching the doors to the case, I drilled for the knobs, which I'd already turned. To install the knobs, I dabbed a little glue in their mortises and used a hand screw to exert pressure on the knob until it was fully seated. I drilled holes in the upper shelf for round magnetic catches and recessed the strikes into the backs of the door stiles.

I applied a thumbnail molding on the front and sides of the bookcase. It is attached to dovetailed keys on the sides (see the photo below), so the molding wouldn't prevent the sides from moving. Once the molding was finished, I sanded the back of the molding flush and sanded the entire top through 320-grit, finishing with 0000 steel wool.

After three coats of Tried and True varnish oil, steel-wooled between coats, the doors were ready for glass. I removed the doors and cut the retainer strips to length, leaving their ends square. Then I predrilled and nailed them in place over the glass with ½-in.-long brass escutcheon pins. After the doors had been rehung, I added leather buttons to the door stops, top and bottom, to deaden the thunk as the doors are shut.

MOLDING IS ATTACHED TO CASE WITH DOVETAIL KEYS. This prevents the case from cracking by letting the side expand and contract.

PETER TURNER

Build a Wall Shelf

My wife, Colleen, occasionally asks me to build a piece of furniture for our home. I would love nothing more than to honor these requests, but there never seems to be time. But a hanging shelf is one project that I figured I could finish quickly.

I got the inspiration from a drawing of a peg-hung Shaker shelf in Ejner Handberg's book, *Shop Drawings of Shaker Furniture and Woodenware*, Vol II (Berkshire Traveller Press, 1975). The shelf sides in Handberg's drawing are curved on top, but the bottom is straight. I added another curve at the bottom, experimenting with different curves until one satisfied my eye. Handberg's Shaker shelves also hung from a wall-mounted peg rail. I don't have a peg rail at home, so the first time I made this piece, I used brass keyhole hangers. In later versions, including the one shown here, I used sim-

SHAKE UP YOUR WALL WITH A SHELF.
This simple wall-hung shelf, perfect for a spice rack or sea shells, was adapted from a traditional Shaker design. The shelves are joined to the sides with sliding dovetails.

pler brass hangers mortised into the second shelf from the top. These are less expensive, easier to install and make hanging the shelf a snap. We use one hanging shelf as a spice rack. The varying heights and sizes of our spice jars helped establish the shelf spacing and overall width.

Consistency is the key to this piece. If you start with flat stock of uniform thickness and length, the joinery follows smoothly. To ensure consistency, do all your milling at once (all the stock is ½ in. thick), and use a plywood pattern and flush-trimming router bit for making identical curved and tapered sides.

The trickiest parts of this piece are the sliding dovetails. Routing the grooves is easy, but the long tails on the ends of each shelf take some patience and finesse. I use a router setup in which the router is mounted horizontally; it seems to make it easier to get a straight, even cut (see the drawing).

By holding the pieces flat on the router table, I have more control as I slide the piece past the bit. I make test pieces out of scrap, which I milled at the same time as the final pieces.

The Shakers housed the shelves in dadoes, rather than sliding dovetails, and you can do the same. It won't be as strong, but if you're worried about the shelves, you can toenail them from the bottom with finish nails or brads.

■ Shaker Shelf Updated

Traditional, peg-hung Shaker wall shelves often have a slight curve at the top and taper from top to bottom. This shelf has a curve at the bottom also, and only the top half is tapered. The piece can be modified by changing the width or the shelf arrangement.

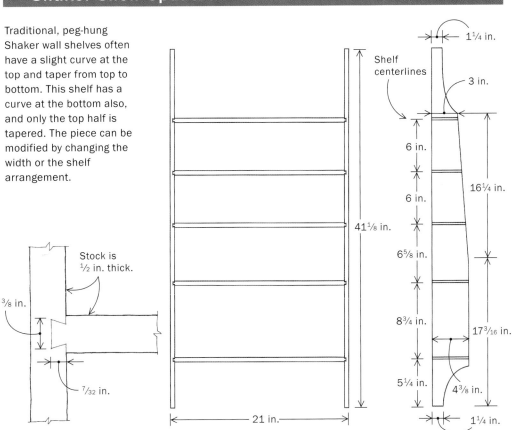

1. Routing dovetail grooves in the sides: After milling all the material to a thickness of ½ in., cut the sides to length, but leave them at least ¼ in. wider than the widest dimension (4⅜ in.). Then mark the centerlines for each shelf on both pieces. Using a slotted piece of plywood to guide a ½-in. router template insert, cut the dovetail slots. First rough the slots with a ¼-in. straight bit, and finish them off with a ⅜-in. dovetail bit.

2. Trace the pattern, and bandsaw the sides: With the grooves routed, cut the curved and tapered sides. First make a plywood pattern matching the shape of the sides of the shelf, trace the pattern onto the back of each side and bandsaw the shape close to the line.

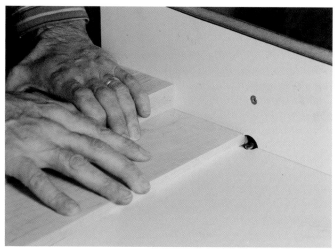

3. Flush-trimming bit makes both sides identical: After roughing out the sides on the bandsaw or jigsaw, clamp each side into the plywood pattern using hold-down clamps fastened to the plywood. Then rout the edge with a ½-in. flush-trimming bit, either using a router table (see the drawing on the facing page) or a hand-held router setup. This step will remove any tearout created when you routed the dovetail grooves, and it makes each side identical.

4. Routing the dovetails on the shelves: To cut the dovetails, mount your router horizontally on the router table (see the drawing on the facing page). This makes it easier to adjust the height of the cut. It also lets you hold the workpiece flat on the table rather than against a fence. Adjust the depth and height of the router bit to match the depth of the slots. I cut the tails to fit by trial and error, testing on scrap stock milled at the same time as the shelf parts.

5. Cut shelves to width and assemble: Don't cut the shelves to width until after you cut the dovetails on the ends, so you can remove any tearout caused by the router. The front edge of the top three shelves is angled to match the tapered sides, which you can do by transferring the angle to the jointer fence. After sanding all the pieces, slide each shelf into the sides, starting at the bottom and clamping each shelf as you go.

HORIZONTAL DOVETAILING FIXTURE MAKES A DIFFICULT JOINT EASY

Cutting sliding dovetails can be tricky. To get a long tail to slide snugly into its groove requires a uniform cut. Rather than holding the shelves vertically to cut the dovetails, you can mount the router horizontally on a standard router table, as shown.

Holding the workpiece flat on the table, cut one side of the tail; then turn the piece over, and cut the other side. Use scrap of the same thickness to establish the exact height and depth of the dovetail bit, and then fit them in a test groove to prevent marring the final pieces.

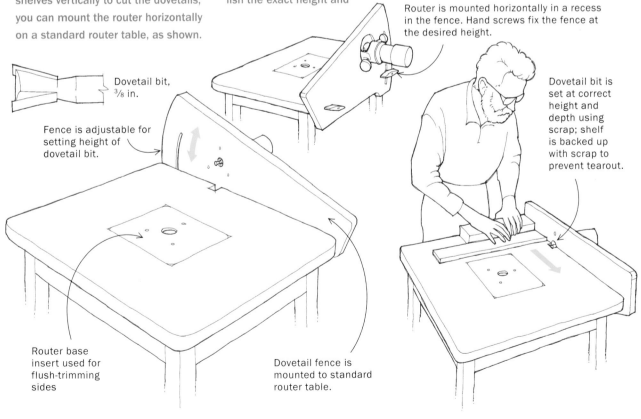

Dovetail bit, ³/₈ in.

Fence is adjustable for setting height of dovetail bit.

Router is mounted horizontally in a recess in the fence. Hand screws fix the fence at the desired height.

Dovetail bit is set at correct height and depth using scrap; shelf is backed up with scrap to prevent tearout.

Router base insert used for flush-trimming sides

Dovetail fence is mounted to standard router table.

CHRIS BECKSVOORT

Desktop Storage

"A PLACE FOR EVERYTHING AND EVERYTHING IN ITS PLACE" was a favorite Shaker sentiment, and this tabletop unit aptly reflects it. This cabinet design also can be customized to suit just about any purpose.

■ Desktop Storage Unit

This small cabinet turns a table into a desk by providing places for stationery, envelopes and bills. Case pieces are ¾ in. thick; all dividers are ⅜ in. thick.

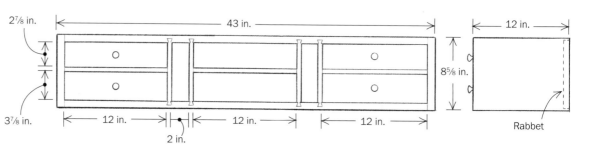

I was sitting at my kitchen table one morning last winter, sipping my Earl Grey tea and surveying the landscape of the tabletop. Stacks of catalogs and magazines dominated. Bills, junk mail and several Christmas cards added to the clutter. A few pens and pencils, my wife's coffee mug and the stamps I hadn't been able to find the afternoon before completed the picture. It was clear to me that some organization was in order. What I needed was a unit that would let me sit at the kitchen table, where I enjoy working, yet still allow me to get organized. I needed a desk that wasn't a desk. So I designed and built one (see the photo on the facing page).

This small cabinet can enhance any workspace, and it isn't difficult to make. Sliding dovetails connect the vertical dividers to the case and stopped dadoes join the horizontal dividers (see the drawing on p. 83). The joinery can be as simple or involved as you wish, and the case can be modified to suit almost any purpose (see the box on p. 84 for a few design ideas).

Once you've figured out the layout and the dimensions, construction is relatively straightforward. For simplicity, I'll describe the construction of the piece shown in the photo on the facing page.

START BY MAKING THE CARCASE

I begin by gluing up stock for the top, bottom and sides. For aesthetic reasons, I use one long board (either one piece of wood or a glued up board) and run the grain up one side, across the top and down the other. The bottom doesn't need to match.

I cut a rabbet for the back of the case in the back inside edges of the top, bottom and sides. To complete the four sides of the carcase, I dovetail the corners. I find that half-blind dovetails (visible from the top and bottom) work best. Because I cut the dovetails and the rabbet for the back to the same depth, I don't have to cut into the dovetails and weaken them.

I omit the half pins at the back of the case; they would be vulnerable because of the stock removed when rabbeting. Instead, I simply square off the last tail at each rear corner (see the drawing on p. 83). The result is a stronger joint. Once all the joints fit snugly, I take the case apart.

DIVIDING THE CASE VERTICALLY WITH SLIDING DOVETAILS

Because this unit is so long and narrow, I thought sliding dovetails would work best as vertical dividers. They lock the top and bottom together and lend the carcase strength and rigidity. These joints are easy to make with a router and router table.

Routing the slots

For the slots, I used a shopmade router fixture (see the drawing and the bottom right photo on p. 80). The fixture consists of two parallel fences, spaced the exact width of the router base, screwed to plywood pieces on both ends. The fixture guides the router so that it makes a dovetailed groove perpendicular to the edge of the workpiece. I have three of these fixtures in different lengths to use on narrow, medium and wide cases.

I lay out the dovetailed slots by clamping the top and bottom case pieces together with their ends flush, and marking the locations for the vertical dividers on their faces and edges. For this piece, I used a ⅜-in. dovetail bit adjusted to a ⅜ in. depth, which is half the thickness of the carcase pieces (see the top left photo on p. 80).

To align the fixture to the layout marks on the carcase pieces, I tack a squared-up piece of pine against the front end of the fixture and rout a slot through it. The piece of pine is brought up flush against the edge of the case and aligned with the marks on the case's edge, which are just visible in the bottom corners of the dovetailed slots (see the bottom left photo on p. 80). This ensures the slot is exactly where it should be. When the fixture is oriented correctly, I clamp it in position and rout across the full width. I repeat the procedure for the other seven slots.

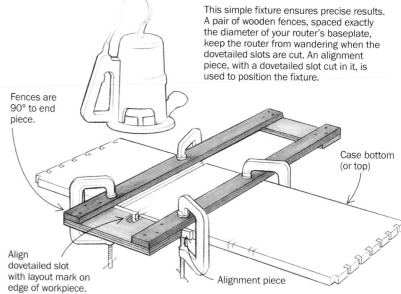

This simple fixture ensures precise results. A pair of wooden fences, spaced exactly the diameter of your router's baseplate, keep the router from wandering when the dovetailed slots are cut. An alignment piece, with a dovetailed slot cut in it, is used to position the fixture.

Fences are 90° to end piece.

Case bottom (or top)

Align dovetailed slot with layout mark on edge of workpiece.

Alignment piece

SET YOUR BIT HEIGHT. For a carcase that's made of ¾-in.-thick stock, set the bit so it's ⅜ in. high. A ruler with graduations on the end works well.

PRECISE ALIGNMENT. Splitting lines on the front edge of the workpiece, visible at the base of the dovetailed slot, ensures dead-on accuracy.

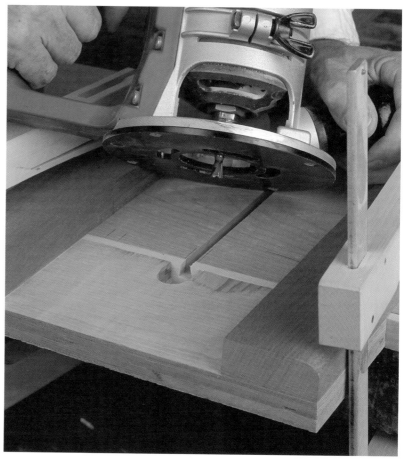

SLIDING DOVETAILS, THE SIMPLE WAY. The fixture keeps the router tracking true; the alignment piece, replaced each time you change bits or depth of cut, makes sure the slot is exactly where you want it.

Routing the dovetails

I make the vertical dividers from ⅜-in.-thick stock. The height is determined by taking the inside dimension of the case and adding ¾ in. (the depth of the two ⅜-in. dovetails, top and bottom). I sand both sides of the dividers and all interior surfaces of the case before measuring for any of the dividers because sanding affects the thickness of the pieces.

I use the same ⅜-in. bit, this time in a router table, and adjust the height to ⅜ in. I make test-cuts in sanded, ⅜-in.-thick scrap, slowly sneaking up on a perfect fit. Remember, you're removing material from both sides of the divider; every time you move the fence, you take off twice that much wood. Be sure to keep the divider pushed tightly against the fence, especially if it has any bow.

Keep testing the fit until the divider slides fully into the slot. It should require only hand pressure, and there should be no gaps or play of any kind. Once the fence is correctly adjusted, repeat the operation for the other three dividers.

DIVIDING THE CASE HORIZONTALLY WITH STOPPED DADOES

Dadoes seem like the best way to divide the case horizontally. I want the piece to look neat, so I use stopped (hidden) dadoes. To mark the positions of the dadoes, I clamp the four vertical dividers between the two ends of the case, supporting the dividers at the bottom with a ⅜-in.-thick piece of scrap. I mark the location of the horizontal dividers and then mark small x's on the front edges of the dividers to indicate where the dadoes will be cut (see the drawing above). An ounce of prevention and all that.

Because the horizontal dividers aren't centered top to bottom on the vertical dividers, I either use two fence settings to cut opposite dadoes (left hand vs. right hand) or use a single fence setting and rely on stops to produce the dadoes safely. I decided on the stops because moving the

Mark dado locations on case sides and dividers with an X.

Case sides

Scrap block, ⅜ in. thick, supports vertical dividers at same height as case bottom.

fence increases the risk of misaligned dadoes. Hand screws work well.

I put a ⅜-in. dado blade in the tablesaw, set the height to ⅛ in. and adjust the fence to match the location of the marks on one of the end pieces. For half the dadoes, I push the workpieces through the blade to a stop that keeps the trailing front edge ¼ in. shy of the dado blade (see the top photo on p. 82). For the other half, I place the back edge of each workpiece on the saw table against a stop. I gently lower the front onto the blade so its end is ¼ in. beyond the dado blade. Then I plow forward to complete the cut (see the bottom photo on p. 82).

I position the stops by making a mark ¼ in. ahead of and behind the blade, placing the workpiece on the stopped blade so that one of its edges lines up with the mark. Then I clamp a hand screw to the saw fence. For the drop cuts, the hand screw prevents kickback; for both the drop and stopped cuts, this technique ensures an accurate ¼-in. stop at one end of the cut.

■ Making stopped dadoes

A HAND SCREW MAKES A GOOD STOP. Dadoes in vertical dividers are stopped ¼ in. shy of the front edge. Because dadoes are not centered on the dividers, there are right- and left-hand pieces. To avoid resetting the fence for facing dadoes, the author cuts half with the hand screw set for a stop cut. Make sure the blade stops before lifting the piece off the table. The other dadoes are made with the hand screw repositioned for a drop cut (below).

DROP CUT GIVES A MIRROR-IMAGE DADO. The author repositions the hand screw on the infeed side of the blade to cut the rest of the dadoes. Each remaining divider is set against the hand screw and lowered carefully into the blade to start the cut. Case ends are cut the same way except that the fence is moved over ⅜ in.

To cut the dadoes in the dividers, I shift the fence toward the blade ⅜ in. This accounts for the height of the dovetails and the depth of the dovetailed slots. I use a chisel to square the fronts of all the dadoes where the blade exits the stock.

ASSEMBLY: ONE STEP AT A TIME

I glue and clamp the main carcase first. After the glue cures, I insert the dovetailed vertical dividers, making sure all corresponding dadoes line up. I slide the dividers in dry about halfway from the front of the case.

Next I apply a thin coating of glue to the front half of the dovetail pins, top and bottom, and to the last few inches of the slots, top and bottom. Applying glue to only part of the joint makes the divider less likely to bind. Then I slide the divider home immediately, getting it flush in the back. The front can always be planed and sanded later. I repeat the process for the remaining three dividers.

I wait to cut the horizontal dividers until after I've assembled the case and can get actual measurements. I plane and cut the dividers to size, notching the corners so they will clear the dado stops. After sanding the horizontal dividers, I slide them halfway into position from the back, lightly glue the back edges of the dividers and then put just a slight smear of glue in the dadoes. This is no place for squeeze-out. Then I slide the dividers quickly home.

After the glue sets up, I plane or sand the front face to be sure that all members are flush and in the same plane.

BACK, DRAWERS, AND FINISHING

The back is constructed like a door. I use thin quartersawn stock for the perimeter frame (see the drawing on the facing page). This virtually eliminates wood movement, which is a good thing because the back is

DESIGN YOUR OWN INSTANT DESK

In designing a desk unit to meet your own needs, start by gathering what you would like to store in it. Stationery, for instance, can easily be housed in a drawer that's 8¾ in. by 11¼ in. This allows room for a standard sheet of paper and clearance to get your finger in and remove a sheet.

A deeper drawer below could have a side-to-side divider for envelopes. And the back half could be further divided for post cards, business cards, checks and the like.

Another drawer could hold a pencil tray. You could even make cutouts for things such as ink bottles, scissors, rulers, fountain pens and drawing instruments. A small, square drawer could be devoted exclusively to computer disks.

Instead of fixed dividers or pigeon holes, you could leave a large opening and include a removable pigeonhole unit—a ⅜-in.-thick bottom with a series of ¼-in.-thick vertical dividers glued into dadoes (see the drawing below). You also might want to incorporate one or more doors with adjustable shelves inside.

If you want to make the unit really portable, mount flush handles on the ends. You could even mount the unit on a wall at a convenient height above a table. All you have to do is make the case ½ in. deeper, recess the back ½ in. and use interlocking cleats. The upper half is mounted to the case, and the lower half is screwed to the wall.

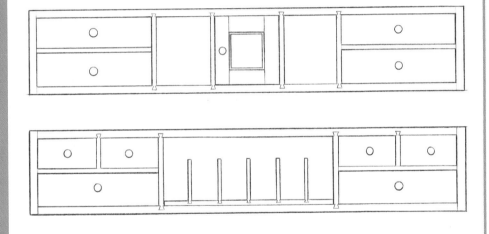

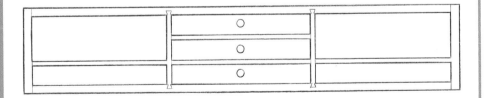

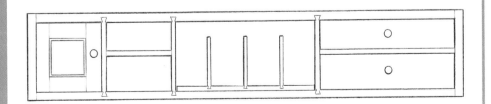

glued into the rabbeted case. The two middle stiles are 4 in. wide, so they span the pigeon holes. The panels are flat and flush with both sides.

After gluing up the back and pinning the mortise-and-tenon joints, I sand the inside faces of the frame and panels and ease all the edges on this assembly. Then I plane the back to fit the rabbeted opening precisely, apply glue to the edges of the back and clamp the back into its opening.

When the assembly is dry, I sand the back, top, bottom and sides to 400-grit and ease all exterior edges. The drawers come last. Then I finish the piece with three coats of Tried & True boiled linseed oil (available from Garrett Wade; 800-221-2942), waiting a day or two between coats. At the four bottom corners, I glue leather pads so the desk unit won't scratch the tabletop.

■ A View from the Back

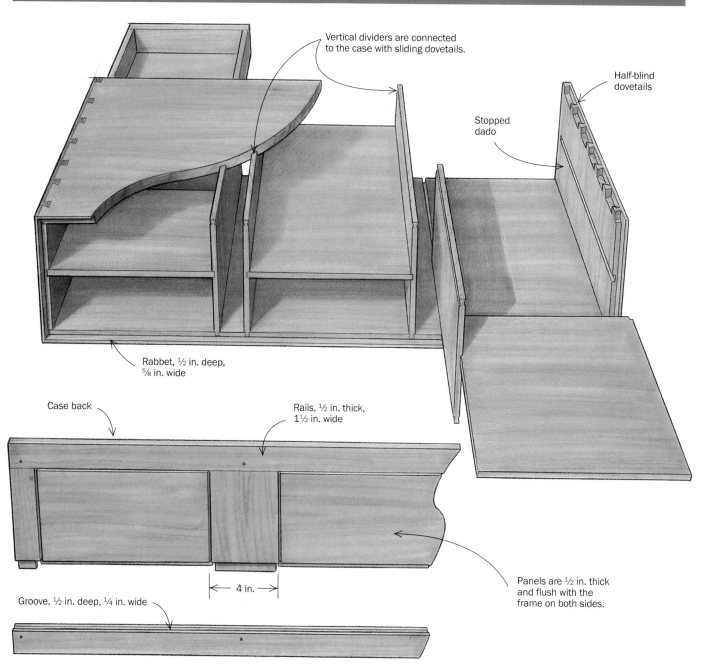

Vertical dividers are connected to the case with sliding dovetails.

Half-blind dovetails

Stopped dado

Rabbet, ½ in. deep, ⅝ in. wide

Case back

Rails, ½ in. thick, 1½ in. wide

← 4 in. →

Groove, ½ in. deep, ¼ in. wide

Panels are ½ in. thick and flush with the frame on both sides.

STEVEN THOMAS BUNN

Workbenches in the Shaker Tradition

I fell in love with Shaker workbenches when I first saw one in Scott Landis' *The Workbench Book* (The Taunton Press, Inc., Newtown, Conn., 1989). I liked the Shaker ideal of "everything neat, orderly and in its place," and the enclosed base, drawers and large top on the bench were exactly what I needed.

The more I thought about the Shaker bench, the more I became aware of the inadequacies of my present bench. Though the top is 24 in. wide, it's still too narrow for the case goods I usually work on. And the tool tray is a catchall for woodchips, sawdust and tools that should have been put away. However, the prospect of building a

THIS SHAKER-STYLE WORK-BENCH offers a large, stable work surface and plenty of storage area built into the base. The main support of the base is four "bents" fashioned after the support system of post-and-beam barns, which allowed the author flexibility in detailing the bases of the benches he built.

bench with a top that resembled an aircraft carrier and enclosed enough storage for a shop full of tools just got added to a long list of dream projects that had little chance of completion.

Several months later, however, dreams became reality. My employer, Thomas Moser, asked me if I would be interested in building a couple of Shaker workbenches. He had been admiring a large bench at the Hancock Shaker Village in Pittsfield, Mass., the very same bench pictured in Landis' book. Moser agreed to provide the materials, do the design work and help as his schedule permitted if I would do most of the actual construction.

BENCH DESIGN

Moser quickly talked me out of slavishly following Landis' plans because we didn't want to duplicate the compromises necessitated by material available to the 19th century. In addition, we each had a different bench in mind. Moser wanted a base with an open center section, so he could sit at the bench while doing design work. The end sections would provide enclosed storage with a bank of drawers in one bay and adjustable shelves fronted by double doors in the other. The back of the bench would be a mirror image of the front.

I like the original benches' two tiers of drawers, side by side, with an open storage section screened by a pair of doors in the end. We both preferred a bench we could work on from all sides, and we wanted the bench to look good from any view.

Because I had to squeeze the benches' construction into downtime at the Moser Cabinetmakers' shops, we wanted to use production methods to streamline parts manufacturing and assembly. We standardized stock dimensions, but we didn't sacrifice construction quality. The resulting frame is strong and massive, yet it still provides flexibility for detailing the drawers and doors to suit each of us.

BUILDING THE BASE

After mulling over these constraints, Moser designed a substantial base framework, as shown in figure 1 on the facing page. A key element of the design is the eight legs that transfer working force from the benchtop directly to the floor. The base was patterned after the timber-framed barns so prevalent in Maine. Four "bents" mortised, tenoned, glued and pinned together are connected by 12 stretchers to form three bays that together are 90 in. long.

I milled the base components from 12/4 cherry. After crosscutting the rough stock to approximate lengths, I jointed one face and ripped the pieces slightly oversized. I then jointed, planed and thickness-sanded the stock to final dimensions, as shown in figure 1 on the facing page. I cut the individual components to length, allowing extra length on the center stiles, rails and stretchers for tenons. After the stock was prepared, I oriented the best face to show and carefully matched grain patterns across the front and rear face of the bench. I marked each piece to maintain grain matching during assembly.

I laid out the mortises on the legs and rails and then cut them on a mortising machine. A plunge router or drill press could be used, but their mortises must be squared up with a chisel or else the tenons will need rounding over to match the mortises.

I cut the tenons $\frac{1}{16}$ in. shorter than the depth of the mortise to allow for glue compression. The stretchers' tenons are even shorter, so they won't bottom out against the cheek of the rails' tenons.

To determine the dimensions for the raised panels, I dry-assembled the base, first fitting the legs, center stiles and rails together to make the bents and then adding the stretchers. After measuring for the panels, I laid out the panel grooves on the frame members. Because Moser's bench was originally designed with an open center bay, I marked grooves on the center bents for panels as well as the end bents.

Fig. 1: Shaker Workbench

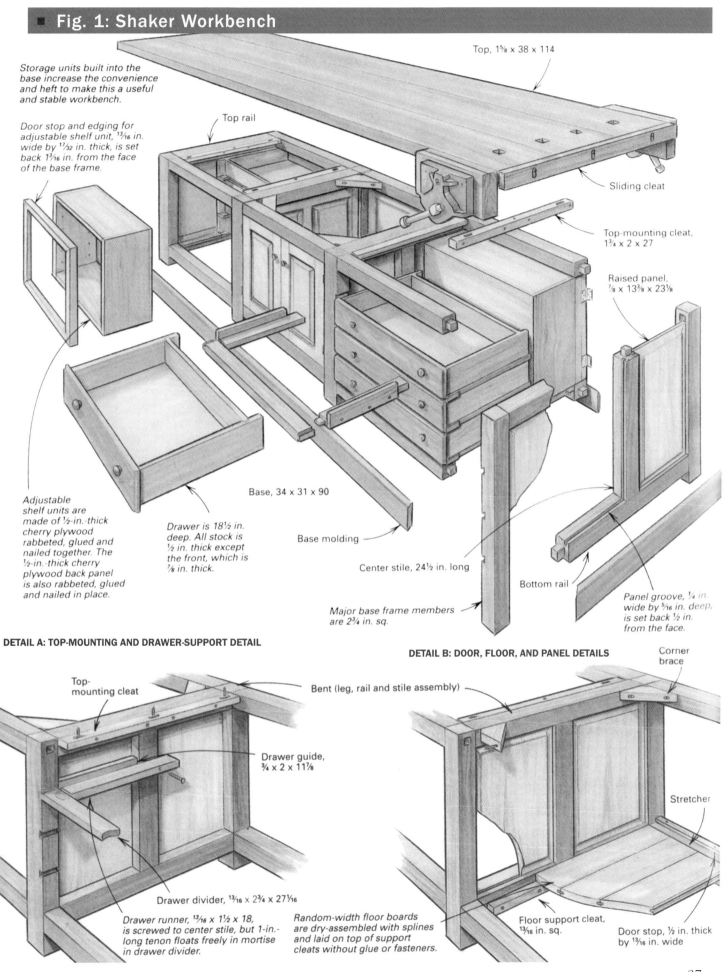

Top, 1⅝ x 38 x 114

Storage units built into the base increase the convenience and heft to make this a useful and stable workbench.

Door stop and edging for adjustable shelf unit, 1³⁄₁₆ in. wide by 1⁷⁄₃₂ in. thick, is set back 1³⁄₁₆ in. from the face of the base frame.

Top rail

Sliding cleat

Top-mounting cleat, 1¾ x 2 x 27

Raised panel, ⅞ x 13⅜ x 23⅛

Adjustable shelf units are made of ½-in.-thick cherry plywood rabbeted, glued and nailed together. The ½-in.-thick cherry plywood back panel is also rabbeted, glued and nailed in place.

Base, 34 x 31 x 90

Drawer is 18½ in. deep. All stock is ½ in. thick except the front, which is ⅞ in. thick.

Base molding

Center stile, 24½ in. long

Bottom rail

Major base frame members are 2¾ in. sq.

Panel groove, ¼ in. wide by ⁵⁄₁₆ in. deep, is set back ½ in. from the face.

Corner brace

DETAIL A: TOP-MOUNTING AND DRAWER-SUPPORT DETAIL

Top-mounting cleat

Bent (leg, rail and stile assembly)

Drawer guide, ¾ x 2 x 11⅞

Stretcher

Drawer divider, 1³⁄₁₆ x 2¾ x 27¹⁄₁₆

Drawer runner, 1³⁄₁₆ x 1½ x 18, is screwed to center stile, but 1-in.-long tenon floats freely in mortise in drawer divider.

Random-width floor boards are dry-assembled with splines and laid on top of support cleats without glue or fasteners.

DETAIL B: DOOR, FLOOR, AND PANEL DETAILS

Floor support cleat, 1³⁄₁₆ in. sq.

Door stop, ½ in. thick by 1³⁄₁₆ in. wide

■ Fig. 2: Routing Dovetail Dadoes

A plywood fence clamped to the bench leg guides the router when cutting dovetail dadoes.

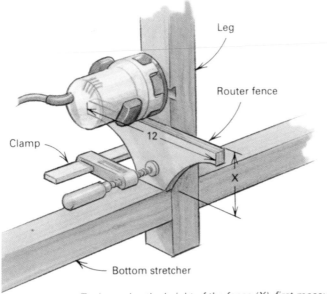

Leg

Router fence

Clamp

12

X

Bottom stretcher

To determine the height of the fence (X), first measure the distance from the bottom stretcher to the centerline of the drawer divider. Then add $\frac{1}{32}$ in. for clearance and subtract the router base radius.

■ Fig. 3: Routing Dovetail Pins

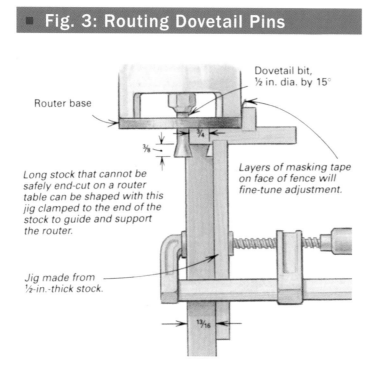

Dovetail bit, $\frac{1}{2}$ in. dia. by 15°

Router base

$\frac{3}{4}$

$\frac{3}{8}$

Long stock that cannot be safely end-cut on a router table can be shaped with this jig clamped to the end of the stock to guide and support the router.

Layers of masking tape on face of fence will fine-tune adjustment.

Jig made from $\frac{1}{2}$-in.-thick stock.

$\frac{13}{16}$

My bench has drawers or doors filling each bay and didn't require the center panels. However, my bench did need the entire back face paneled because it doesn't have doors or drawers as Moser's does. I then disassembled the base and plowed the panel grooves with a dado blade on my tablesaw. I didn't worry about stopping the grooves on the legs because the base molding would hide the exposed grooves at the bottom of the leg.

Raised panels were made from 5/4 stock thicknessed to ⅞ in. I cut the bevel at 30° and left the field raised ⅛ in. higher than the bevel. Finally, after several months of interrupted work, I glued and assembled the base components. The face of the field is flush with the face of the legs when the panel is installed in its grooves.

THE TOP

Because I needed my bench as a work surface, I began making the tops before final detailing of the base. I glued up the top from 8/4 cherry stock that was planed to 1¾ in. thick and then thickness-sanded to 1⅝ in. I trimmed the tops to length and screwed them in place using a cleat at each bent, as shown in figure 1 on p. 87.

To finish Moser's benchtop, I bolted on two Record model 52D vises, one on each side opposing each other at one end of the top. Moser also added sliding cleats on each end of his bench, which can be pulled up to serve as stops when planing or beltsanding stock on the benchtop. A few dog holes drilled across the top between the two vises completed his top. I bolted a vise to the left end of my top and later added a section along the front edge to include a tail vise.

BUILDING IN STORAGE SPACE

My bench, with its two banks of drawers and the open bay with doors, was the easiest to complete because the storage was only accessible from the front of the bench. I made my drawers 24 in. deep and extended the sides 6 in. past the drawer back. The extended sides let me pull the drawer out to its full length without the drawer falling out.

The open bay needs only a floor and a pair of doors hung from the legs of the bents on either side. The floor is simply random widths of cherry boards, splined together and loosely laid onto ledger strips screwed to the bottom rails and stretchers. I left about ⅛-in. gap between boards for seasonal expansion. I filled in the bench's back side with raised panels for a finished appearance from all sides.

Moser's storage system was a little more complex because he wanted storage on both sides of the bench. The drawers on one side are backed up by adjustable shelves on the other side, as shown in figure 1 on p. 87. The drawer units are made the same as mine, but they are only about 20 in. deep to allow space for the adjustable shelving on the opposite side. The adjustable shelving is made as a separate unit that slides into place between the bents and is screwed into place. I then screwed some trim around the front edge of the shelving unit, which hid the raw plywood edge and also serves as door stops.

ADDING THE DRAWER DIVIDERS

To support the drawers, I added dividers, runners and guides as shown in figure 1 on p. 87. Sliding dovetails secure each drawer divider to the legs and add more strength to the massive base. I routed the dovetail pins on the ends of the dividers guided by a jig. I routed their corresponding dadoes on the legs guided by fences made of ¼-in.-thick scrap plywood, as shown in figure 2 on the facing page. I made three fences of different heights, one for each dado in a leg. The

DRAWERS ARE SUPPORTED by a runner that is mortised and tenoned to the drawer divider and then screwed to the center stile. A drawer guide screwed to the runner keeps the drawer aligned for easy closing.

I improvised a method of creating a thumbnail molding on the drawer fronts for this bench using my router and tablesaw because that was what I had available. The thumbnail extends past the drawer opening on three sides (top, left and right) but is flush with the opening at the bottom of the drawer, even though the profile is the same all around the drawer. I'd seen this detailing on an antique piece and decided to try it on my bench. The technique is simple, works well and should be of interest to any woodworker who doesn't own a shaper but would like to be able to detail drawers, as shown in the photo at right. The same procedures will also produce drawer fronts lipped on all four sides.

RADIUS THE EDGE

I started with drawer-front blanks that were $\frac{5}{8}$ in. wider than the drawer opening (to allow $\frac{1}{4}$ in. overlap at each end, plus $\frac{1}{16}$ in. for waste) and $\frac{3}{8}$ in. oversize from top to bottom (to allow $\frac{1}{4}$-in. overlap at the top and

$\frac{1}{16}$-in. waste at the top and bottom). If you want a lipped edge on all four sides of the drawer front, the blank should be $\frac{5}{8}$ in. higher than the opening as well as $\frac{5}{8}$ in. wider. After dimensioning the drawer fronts, I chose the best face of each drawer front, and then I routed a $\frac{3}{8}$-in. radius on all four edges of each, leaving a $\frac{1}{16}$-in. fillet. You can rout this radius freehand with a hand-held router and a bearing-guided bit as I did, or you can use a router table, if you prefer, for greater stability.

CREATE THE END LIPS

The next step was to create the lip along the top and both ends of the drawer. I set the fence on my tablesaw so that the far side of the blade was $\frac{5}{16}$ in. away, and I set the blade height at $\frac{17}{32}$ in. ($\frac{1}{2}$ in. to create the shoulder for the half-blind dovetails plus $\frac{1}{32}$-in. clearance). Holding the drawer front in place with my miter gauge, I made a first pass to establish the shoulder and then made several more passes to remove

THE THUMBNAIL MOLDING AROUND THE DRAWER FRONTS adds just a bit of restrained ornament to this well-designed but utilitarian bench. The molding is easily cut with router and tablesaw.

waste, moving the drawer front steadily away from the fence. For this operation, it's okay to use the miter gauge in conjunction with the fence because there is no cutoff to jam between blade and fence or to be thrown back at you. After doing one end of each drawer front, I repeated the procedure on the other end. An important feature to note is that the drawer shrinks approximately ¹⁄₁₆ in. in length at each end as a result of the blade removing the very tips of the radius.

CREATING THE TOP LIP

With the blade height unchanged, I reset my fence to 4¹⁵⁄₁₆ in. away from the blade for these 5¼-in.-high drawers. Generically speaking, you want to set the fence at ⁵⁄₁₆ in. less than your final drawer height. This takes into account the ¹⁄₁₆ in. you're going to lose at the top of the drawer front when the blade cuts away the tip of the radius. Make your cut, and then move the fence away from the blade ⅛ in. at a time, making repeated passes until you've cut away the waste to create the top lip of the drawer edge.

TRIMMING THE DRAWER BOTTOM

To establish the same thumbnail reveal on the drawer front's bottom edge, I set the fence at 5¼ in. for these drawers (final width, however wide your drawers are). Then I raised the blade enough to clear the edge of the drawer front and made the cut. This cut takes another ¹⁄₁₆ in. off the bottom, visually balancing the drawer. For drawers lipped on all four edges, reset the fence to ⁵⁄₁₆ in. less than final drawer height and repeat the steps when creating the top lip.

These drawings present a step-by-step procedure for shaping thumbnail moldings with a router and tablesaw. (Drawing headings are keyed to bold headings in the text.)

RADIUS THE EDGE

Top of drawer front

Radius, ⅜ in.

¹⁄₁₆

**CREATE THE END LIPS:
ESTABLISH THE SHOULDER**

Tablesaw fence

¹⁷⁄₃₂

⁵⁄₁₆

Sawblade

REMOVE WASTE

Using miter gauge as a guide, move drawer front over ⅛ in. each pass until waste is removed. Clean up lip with a rabbet plane.

CREATING THE TOP LIP

Move fence over ⅛ in. each pass until waste is removed.

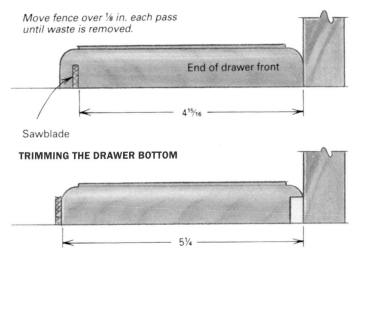

End of drawer front

4¹⁵⁄₁₆

Sawblade

TRIMMING THE DRAWER BOTTOM

5¼

fences register off the bottom stretcher and ensure that the dadoes are spaced properly without measuring. I clamped a fence to a leg and then routed the dovetail dado in a single pass at full depth with a ¾-in.-dia., 15° dovetail bit. This technique can cause tearout though, so you may want to hog out the waste by making progressively deeper passes with a straight bit before routing with the dovetail bit.

When the dadoes were completed, I cut the divider to length and dovetailed the ends. I used the jig shown in figure 3 on p. 88 to cut the pins. I clamped the jig to the end of the divider, and then I made a pass with a 15° dovetail bit in a small router. I turned the jig around and made a second pass on the other side of the divider to complete the dovetail pin. Before installing the drawer divider, I mortised the back edge to accept sliding tenons on the drawer runners. The floating tenon accommodates any seasonal wood movement in the base structure.

I installed the dividers and then added the runners by slipping their tenoned ends into mortises in the dividers. Then I screwed the runner to the center stile of each bent. To make drawer movement easier, I attached guides to the runners to restrict the drawer's side-to-side movement.

MAKING THE DRAWERS

All drawer components are made of cherry. The bottom is beveled at 15° on three sides to fit a ⁵⁄₁₆-in.-wide groove in the drawer front and sides. The bottom is glued into the front groove. A slot in the bottom allows me to screw the bottom to the drawer back and still lets the bottom float freely for expansion and contraction caused by changes in humidity.

The drawers are dovetailed together; half-blind dovetails at the front and sliding dovetails at the back. The sliding dovetail dado is cut with a ½-in.-dia. dovetail bit set ¼ in. deep. I cut the dovetail pins on both ends of the back on a router table.

To dress up the face of the bench and to make the drawers a little easier to fit, I used a thumbnail-shaped overlapping edge on the drawer fronts. Although thumbnail bits are available, I couldn't find one of the appropriate size for my drawers. Instead of having a custom bit ground, I used a combination of a ⅜-in.-radius roundover bit and my tablesaw to create the desired shape as discussed in the box on the facing page. After shaping the drawer face, I used a router jig to cut the half-blind dovetails to join the front to the sides.

FRAME-AND-PANEL DOORS

The remaining open bays and the adjustable shelves were enclosed with frame-and-panel doors inset into the openings. The door frames are joined with pegged mortises and tenons. The rails and stiles are made with 1⅛-in.-thick stock to accommodate the ¹⁵⁄₁₆-in.-thick panel with the same 30° raised-panel bevel as those on the rest of the bench.

Once my bench was completed, Moser preferred the appearance of the drawers and doors across the front to his bench with the open center bay. I added a pair of doors to both sides to close in the center bay and give him the look he liked. The doors can be opened for leg room.

The finishing touch is the 4-in.-wide baseboard I counterbored, screwed and plugged around the bottom of the base. I mitered the corners and then routed a ⅜-in.-wide bead in the top edge of the molding.

IAN INGERSOLL

Break Out of the Bathroom Vanity Box

Lately I've grown tired of vanity cabinets. Apparently I'm not alone, because in catalogs and showrooms, I see more and more bathroom furniture: table-like vanities, stand-alone cabinets, little stands for serving up towels. But I didn't arrive at my design from the ranks of the avant-garde; rather, this vanity, with its gently tapered and splayed legs, is an outgrowth of years of working in the Shaker tradition.

I see it as a forward-looking nod to the Shaker washstand. I've also grown tired of cherry, a wood I feel furniture makers have worked to death. I made this vanity out of walnut, and a cheap grade at that, oxidized a deep, mocha brown with potassium permanganate (see the box on p. 99). The vanity base fits comfortably under a solid-surface top and relies on a few simple design moves and the striking ebony-like finish. With this design, you won't need a fat wallet to make your bathroom look like a million bucks.

In designing the vanity, I had to consider a few issues particular to the genre. For height, I went with a fairly standard 33 in. For width, a 34-in. top felt right, and it allowed for two narrow drawers, one to either side of the bowl. The one caveat is that 34 in. is not a standard top size. You could adapt my design for either a 31-in. top or a 37-in. top, the two standard sizes closest to 34 in. Or you could have the top custom fabricated (see the box on p. 95), as

I did. Regardless of the width you choose, you may need a custom top to get one without the standard-issue integral backsplash.

All vanity tops are 22 in. deep, so to determine the overhang and the ultimate width of the table, I had to work back from 22 in. The key is to allow enough overhang in the rear so that the backsplash will sit flush against the wall and the legs will leave room for baseboard molding (see the drawing on p. 96).

Even a vanity-as-table benefits from storage space. So I insisted on the two drawers, and I included a grate for a shelf. I'd used a similar floating grate on a kitchen island, and it seemed just right for this vanity.

To accommodate plumbing, I made the aprons deep enough to hide the sink bowl and most of the trap; a little chrome plumbing showing underneath keeps the vanity honest. You or your plumber can relocate the supply lines to run through or just below the rear apron. Either way, you won't see them from the front. As for moisture, a few coats of polyurethane over the permanganate finish should protect the wood surfaces for years. And compared with a closed-in cabinet, the open design of the legs and grate allow plenty of air circulation.

Constructing the vanity requires a trick or two, but it isn't difficult or especially time-consuming if you take it in stages.

■ The front apron

RIP AND REGLUE TO CRAFT A FRONT APRON WITH FLUSH DRAWERS. Rip the apron at the top and bottom of the drawers (right). After jointing the ripped edges, cut the middle piece to make two drawer fronts; then glue and clamp the apron pieces together again (far right). Cut the apron to length after glue-up. With a saw set to cut at 2°, mark the length at the top of the apron (bottom left). After the apron is glued in place, mark the upper outside corner of the drawer fronts, and cut them to length with the saw set at 2° (bottom right).

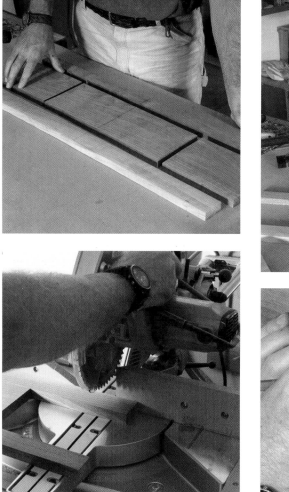

Easy for me to say, since Pieter Mulder, one of the craftsmen I employ, built the prototype for me. But I think Pieter would agree.

VANITY IS A TABLE

Not counting the floating grate (see the box on p. 97) or the backsplash, the essence of the vanity is four legs and four aprons, plus the two drawers. Make them in that order.

I needed to leave a full 16 in. for the sink bowl, which necessitated pushing the drawers against the tapered legs. An angled drawer front is scarcely harder to make than a straight-sided drawer front, and the slim line between the drawer front and the leg helps you read the legs as splayed, even though the angle is a mere 2°. I had a guy working for me a while back, and his first run of supposedly vertical tables turned out splayed: He called it his fat-boy line of furniture, because it looked like someone heavy had sat on the tables. With the vanity, I intended the splay.

Mill the legs square, and then cut the tapers. The taper on both the inside faces of the legs runs straight from the bottom of the apron to the foot of the leg (see the drawing on p. 96). Save the scraps from your ripcuts, and use them later as clamping pads when gluing the aprons to the legs. Cut the mortises perpendicular to the inside faces of the legs.

Mill the aprons long, and cut them to length with a chop saw set at 2° off vertical. To figure the finished length of each apron, determine the distance between the legs at the top, and add 1⅜ in. on each side for tenons; for instance, Pieter cut the side aprons 17¾ in. long.

Before cutting the tenons, you need to rip and reglue the front apron for the two flush drawers. The front apron needs to begin a bit wider and longer than the other aprons because you'll lose two sawkerfs when you cut out the drawer fronts (see the photos on the facing page). Rip the apron proud of your lines, so you can joint the fresh edges before glue-up. The reglued

apron will have a very close grain match despite the missing kerfs. Once the front apron has been glued together again, you can joint all four aprons at the same time.

Now you can cut all the tenons. Use a tablesaw with a dado set, cutting the shoulders first with the board flat over the dado set. Then cut the cheeks using a miter gauge, with the boards standing on edge. Because the shoulders are cut 2° off vertical, cutting the cheeks on edge will leave a triangle that must be pared out by hand.

Once you've cut the legs and aprons, you're ready to glue up the table. Leave the aprons a touch proud of the legs, and scrape and sand them flush. If, instead, the

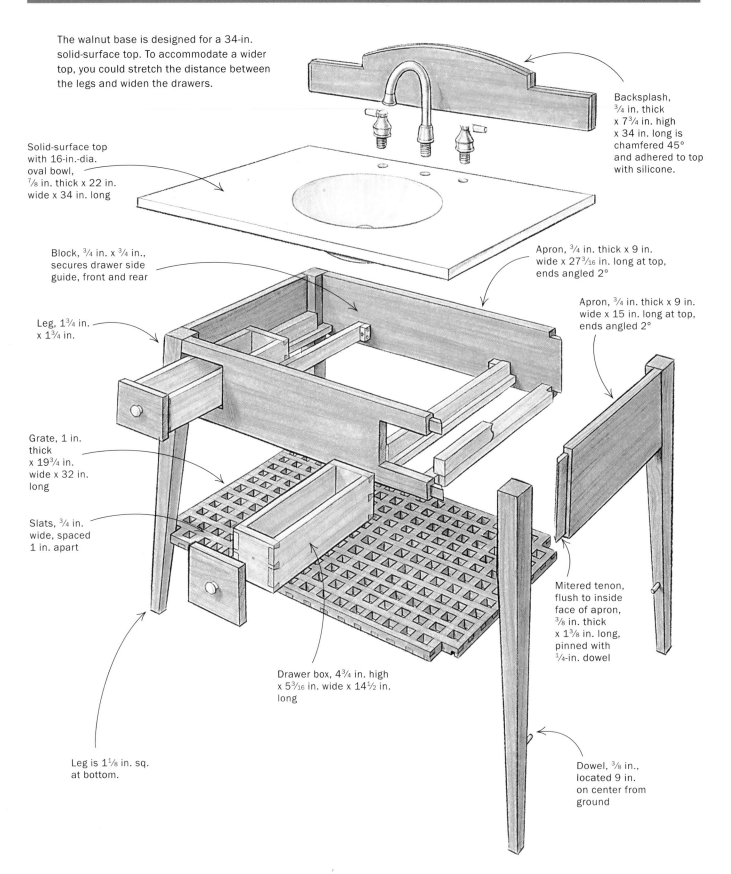

The walnut base is designed for a 34-in. solid-surface top. To accommodate a wider top, you could stretch the distance between the legs and widen the drawers.

Backsplash, ³/₄ in. thick x 7³/₄ in. high x 34 in. long is chamfered 45° and adhered to top with silicone.

Solid-surface top with 16-in.-dia. oval bowl, ⁷/₈ in. thick x 22 in. wide x 34 in. long

Block, ³/₄ in. x ³/₄ in., secures drawer side guide, front and rear

Apron, ³/₄ in. thick x 9 in. wide x 27³/₁₆ in. long at top, ends angled 2°

Apron, ³/₄ in. thick x 9 in. wide x 15 in. long at top, ends angled 2°

Leg, 1³/₄ in. x 1³/₄ in.

Grate, 1 in. thick x 19³/₄ in. wide x 32 in. long

Slats, ³/₄ in. wide, spaced 1 in. apart

Mitered tenon, flush to inside face of apron, ³/₈ in. thick x 1³/₈ in. long, pinned with ¹/₄-in. dowel

Drawer box, 4³/₄ in. high x 5³/₁₆ in. wide x 14¹/₂ in. long

Leg is 1¹/₈ in. sq. at bottom.

Dowel, ³/₈ in., located 9 in. on center from ground

leg is proud of the apron, you'll run into trouble because you'll lose the crisp line of the leg as you sand it down. The 2° taper on the aprons will transfer to the legs, so you may want to beltsand or plane the tops of the legs flush with the top edges of the aprons. Sanding the legs flush with the apron will help the vanity top to sit flat. One thing nice about the splayed legs and the floating grate is that you don't have to include the grate in the glue-up.

You can build the two drawer boxes any way you like; just be sure the inner sides avoid the sink bowl. Wait until the table is glued up to cut the drawer front to length. Mark the length of the top edge against the drawer opening, and use this mark to make a 2° cut.

Making the wood grate takes less time than you might think, as long as you don't attempt to cut and notch each piece individually. The trick is to cut a series of dadoes, half the thickness of the board, across a wide 1-in.-thick board. Then rip the board, which results in several identically notched strips indexed to fit together when arranged in a grid.

For a grate that appears to float around the legs, first make a full rectangular grid and then cut away the corners with a jigsaw. Chisel the inside faces clean. The assembled grate can be sanded with a belt sander or sent through a thickness sander.

I considered several ways of attaching the grate to the legs, but settled on resting the grate on four dowels, one protruding from each leg (see the photo at right). With a ½-in. reveal between the grate and the legs and with the dowels half-hidden in notches in the underside of the grate, anyone walking up to the vanity will perceive the grate as floating. (Those who get down on their hands and knees and crawl around on your bathroom floor will have earned the right to know how the grate is attached.) Use ⅜-in. wood or metal dowels, set ⅝ in. into the leg and protrud-

ing 1 in. Be sure to drill the hole for the dowel parallel to the vanity top, not perpendicular to the splayed and tapered leg.

PUTTING A LID ON IT

Once you've assembled the legs and aprons, fitted the drawers and built the grate, you're almost done. The next-to-last step is to install the solid-surface top onto the wood table. It's almost a non-event, a task best left undone until you're actually plumbing the vanity. A solid-surface top is quite heavy— it tends to stay where you put it—and the

■ Getting the Rear Overhang Right

The solid-surface vanity top needs to overhang the base at the rear by 2 in. to allow ¾ in. between the leg and the wall for a baseboard.

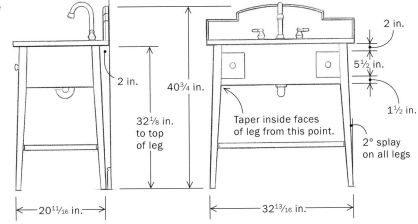

2 in.

40¾ in.

32⅛ in. to top of leg

20¹¹⁄₁₆ in.

32¹³⁄₁₆ in.

2 in.

5½ in.

1½ in.

Taper inside faces of leg from this point.

2° splay on all legs

FIRST CROSS-DADO A LONG BLANK USING A SIMPLE JIG. With this jig, you'll be able to index a series of consistent dadoes across a 1-in.-thick by 3-in.- or 4-in.-wide board.

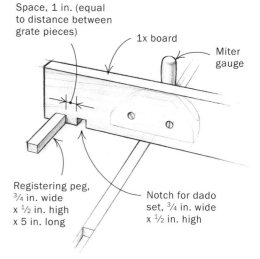

Space, 1 in. (equal to distance between grate pieces)

1x board

Miter gauge

Registering peg, ¾ in. wide x ½ in. high x 5 in. long

Notch for dado set, ¾ in. wide x ½ in. high

RIP THE BLANK INTO NOTCHED STRIPS. When you rip a really wide board into narrow strips, you have many chances to kick the board off square as you pass it through the saw, resulting in tapered strips that don't fit well together. You're better off ripping boards that are 3 in. or 4 in. wide.

wood table needs to move under it, so the barest of connections is required. Simply run a bead of silicone along the top edge of the front apron, and lay the solid-surface top in place.

The backsplash is shaped from a 7¾-in.-wide piece of walnut. Cut it with a bandsaw, clean it up and then use a chamfer bit on your router to bevel the edge.

The final step, I promise, is to attach the backsplash to the solid-surface top. With the vanity in place, affix the backsplash to the rear wall with silicone, and run a bead of caulk between the backsplash and vanity top. Now you can admire your work, and then wash your hands.

A RICH FINISH FOR POOR WOOD

There are any number of disaster stories associated with the use of potassium permanganate as a finish, most having to do with turning something black that wasn't supposed to be.

A chemical that oxidizes wood to change its color, potassium permanganate is sold in water-soluble salt form. It is considered a toxin, though it is neither volatile, flammable nor listed as a carcinogen. You should wear a respirator when mixing the salts and gloves when applying the finish. You may have luck purchasing potassium permanganate from a local water conditioning company, such as Culligan. One mail-order supplier of potassium permanganate is Olde Mill Cabinet Shoppe (717-755-8884). Ask for a Material Safety Data Sheet (MSDS), and expect to pay a hazardous-materials shipping charge.

Potassium permanganate reacts differently to different woods and at different dilutions, so always test it on some scrap. It dries in one to two hours, and it is very forgiving and uniform in darker shades, making it a good choice for inexpensive, poor quality woods, such as sappy walnut.

For the vanity, David Blakey, one of the finishers at my shop, applied three coats of potassium permanganate (1 tablespoon mixed with 1 quart of water) and then two coats of Minwax Polyshade, urethane with a tint to prevent UV damage to the oxidized finish.

ROBERT TREANOR

Shaker Tall Clock

Order, punctuality and the timely completion of tasks were the rules of the day in Shaker communities. Even so, watches were considered inappropriate under the dictates of the faith. Tall clocks as well as wall-hung clocks were another story. They readily found a place in the community dwelling houses of the Shakers. Usually found in central hallways, tall clocks could be viewed easily by Shaker brothers and sisters as they went about their chores.

Shaker clocks, especially tall clocks, are most often associated with the Watervliet community in upstate New York. This is where Benjamin Youngs, a skilled clockmaker, became a convert to Shakerism. Youngs had been an apprentice to his father, a clockmaker in Hartford, Conn. Benjamin converted to the Shaker faith after he moved his family to a farm near the Watervliet community.

Brother Benjamin's early clocks, made before and shortly after his conversion, show an awareness of the fashion of the day. After his conversion, his clocks have the straightforward, functional and modest properties associated with Shaker design.

■ Building the case

CASE JOINERY IS SIMPLE.
Sides are glued and nailed
into rabbets cut in the case
front. The back is screwed on,
and the case is joined to the
base with glue dowels.

DOWELING JIG. Holes bored in a hardwood
scrap guide the bit as the author drills out a
case side for glue dowels.

FLIP JIG, AND DRILL BOTTOM. The jig, with
its fence removed, is flipped over and
aligned with layout lines on the case bottom to drill matching holes.

TEST-FIT. The jig ensures that dowels line
up correctly, even if guide holes are not perfectly spaced or centered.

YOU DON'T NEED HARD-TO-FIND STOCK

The clock shown on p. 101 is based on one
that's believed to be the work of Benjamin
Youngs. That clock is illustrated in John
Kassay's *The Book of Shaker Furniture*
(University of Massachusetts Press, 1980).
Kassay's measured drawings, in meticulous
detail, give accurate dimensions of the parts
down to a thirty-second of an inch. I modified the dimensions slightly, so I could get
the required parts from clear pine in nomi-
nal 1 in. thicknesses.

I can make this clock from standard lumberyard material, surfaced on all four sides
(S4S), with only a small amount of waste.
It pays to take your time at the lumberyard
when selecting stock. Because some pieces,
like the case front, are made with the full
width of standard dimensioned material,
you should pick only stock with straight,
parallel sides. It's a good idea to take a
straightedge with you to make sure the
material is flat across its face.

The original clock was made with pine,
and so is this one. The front and back of
the case are made from 1x12s. The remaining parts are made from standard 1x10 and
1x8 pine. A painted finish is simple and
authentic. I've also used hardwood with a
clear finish.

CASE JOINERY IS SIMPLE BUT STRONG

I begin construction of the clock case by
ripping the 6¼-in. sides from 1x10s, saving
the rippings for later use. After carefully
squaring the sides to length, I make a simple doweling jig (see top left photo) from
some square ¾-in. by ¾-in. material. The
outside faces of the case sides must be
exactly 11¼ in. apart. By orienting the jig
along baselines accurately laid out on the
case bottom and across the end grain of the
case sides, I can bore holes guaranteed to
align (see center left photo). A stop on the
drill bit prevents boring all the way through
the bottom. I use ⅜-in. dowels, cutting them

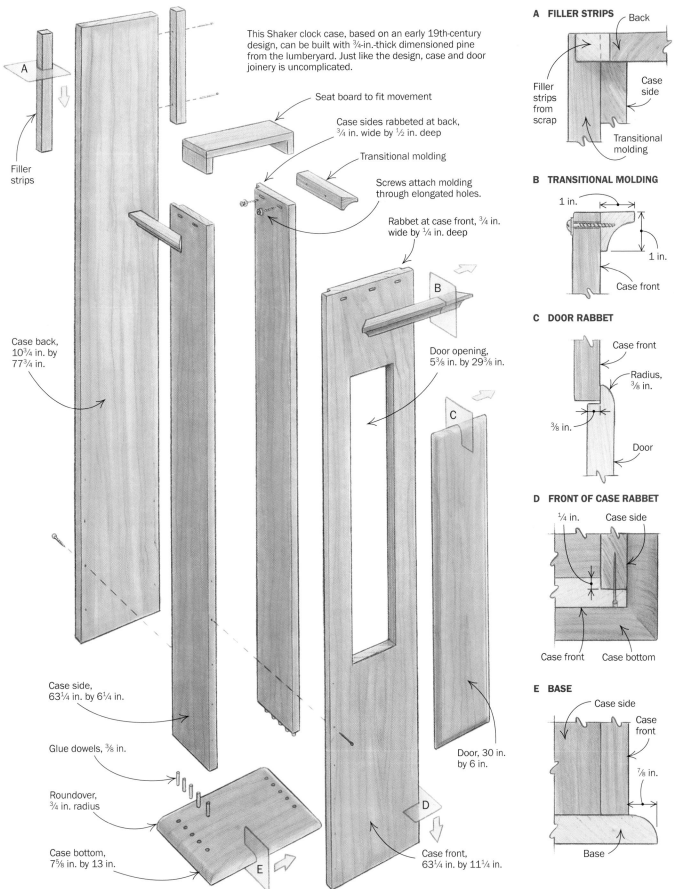

This Shaker clock case, based on an early 19th-century design, can be built with ¾-in.-thick dimensioned pine from the lumberyard. Just like the design, case and door joinery is uncomplicated.

Seat board to fit movement

Case sides rabbeted at back, ¾ in. wide by ½ in. deep

Transitional molding

Screws attach molding through elongated holes.

Rabbet at case front, ¾ in. wide by ¼ in. deep

Door opening, 5⅜ in. by 29⅜ in.

Filler strips

Case back, 10¾ in. by 77¾ in.

Case side, 63¼ in. by 6¼ in.

Glue dowels, ⅜ in.

Roundover, ¾ in. radius

Case bottom, 7⅝ in. by 13 in.

Door, 30 in. by 6 in.

Case front, 63¼ in. by 11¼ in.

A FILLER STRIPS

Back

Filler strips from scrap

Case side

Transitional molding

B TRANSITIONAL MOLDING

1 in.

1 in.

Case front

C DOOR RABBET

Case front

Radius, ⅜ in.

⅜ in.

Door

D FRONT OF CASE RABBET

¼ in.

Case side

Case front

Case bottom

E BASE

Case side

Case front

⅞ in.

Base

SLIDE-ON BONNET. The bonnet for this Shaker tall clock rests on transitional molding at the top of the case. It slides on and off to provide access to the clock's movement.

BONNET CONSTRUCTION

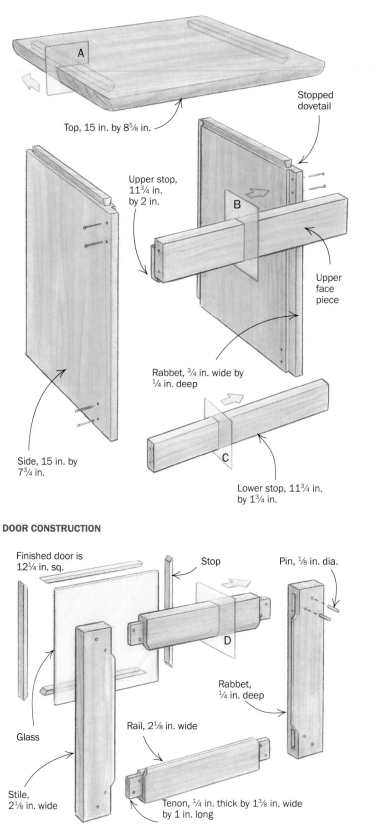

Top, 15 in. by 8⅝ in.

Stopped dovetail

Upper stop, 11¾ in. by 2 in.

Upper face piece

Rabbet, ¾ in. wide by ¼ in. deep

Side, 15 in. by 7¾ in.

Lower stop, 11¾ in. by 1¾ in.

DOOR CONSTRUCTION

Finished door is 12¼ in. sq.

Stop

Pin, ⅛ in. dia.

Rabbet, ¼ in. deep

Glass

Rail, 2⅛ in. wide

Stile, 2⅛ in. wide

Tenon, ¼ in. thick by 1⅜ in. wide by 1 in. long

A   SLIDING DOVETAIL

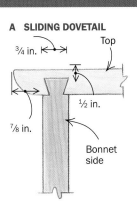

¾ in.

Top

½ in.

⅞ in.

Bonnet side

B   DOOR STOP

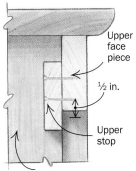

Upper face piece

½ in.

Upper stop

Bonnet side

C   LOWER DOOR STOP

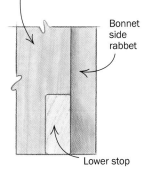

Bonnet side

Bonnet side rabbet

Lower stop

D   BONNET DOOR

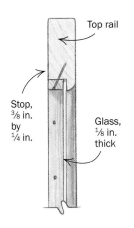

Top rail

Stop, ⅜ in. by ¼ in.

Glass, ⅛ in. thick

to length carefully so they don't bottom out in the holes.

The front of the case is made from the full width of a 1x12, which is actually 11¼ in. I attach the front to the sides with a nailed and glued rabbet joint. I often cut the rabbet at the tablesaw with a ¾-in.-wide dado head. But for this case, I used a router with a rabbeting bit. The rabbet is cut ¼ in. deep and runs the entire length of the front. Then I cut out the opening for the case door with a hand-held scroll saw at the bench.

While the dado head is still in the saw, I cut rabbets in the back edge of the case sides to accommodate the back. I keep the width at ¾ in., but I increase the depth to ½ in. (I leave the back thickness at ¾ in., though it easily can be reduced to ½ in.) I rip the back to width from a 1x12. Ultimately, I will screw the back onto the case. Before doing so, I attach narrow filler strips, cut from the side rippings, to the top to span the gap created by the difference in width between the case and the hood.

GLUING UP THE CASE AND APPLYING THE MOLDING

Before gluing the case together, I round over the front and ends of the case bottom with a ¾-in.-radius router bit. I also give all case parts a preliminary sanding. You'll need a few long bar clamps to glue the dowel joints at the bottom of the case. The front is glued and nailed, and the back is simply screwed on. The front and back will help to hold the assembly square while the glue has time to dry. After the glue has dried and the nail holes have been filled, the case can be given its final sanding.

There was one part of this clock I couldn't cut from my standard material: the transitional cove molding attached to the top of the case. But in keeping with the frugal nature of this exercise, I took the molding from some rippings left over from a Windsor chair seat blank. I cut the molding profile with a ¾-in.-radius cove bit in the router. For safety's sake, I left the blank wide, cut the profile and then ripped the molding to width.

FOR CLEAN MITERS, USE A GUIDE. Rabbets on door stiles and rails meet in a miter at inside corners. For tight-fitting joints, the author pares pieces with the help of a guide block cut to a 45° angle.

CLAMP AND PARE. With the rabbet cut away at the end of the door stile, the author pares the miter with a sharp chisel. The mitering template is clamped to the stile along the layout line.

Of the myriad ways to attach the molding, my choice was one of the simplest: gluing the miters and screwing the length of the molding to the case through slotted holes from the inside. Although there's no guarantee the miters will never open up, the slotted holes give the case a way to expand and contract seasonally without cracking. The case door is lipped and rabbeted all the way around and attached with offset hinges, like those often found on kitchen cabinets.

SLIDING DOVETAILS JOIN HOOD TOP AND SIDES

As in most tall clocks, the hood of this one is removable, providing access to the movement. After double-checking the dimensions, I cut the sides and top of the hood from a length of 1x10. The joint of the side to top easily could be the dowel joint used in the case, but for variety, I used a sliding dovetail on this clock (see the drawings on pp. 104-105). Easily cut with a router inverted in a table, the sliding dovetail is a strong and appropriate joint.

Location of the joint is critical. The outside face of the hood sides must line up with the outside edge of the transitional molding. I mark the location of the joint on the underside of the hood top and set the height of the ¾-in. dovetail bit at ½ in. Then I carefully adjust the fence on the router table. With soft pine, there is no need to plow out a dado before cutting the dovetail; the joint is cut with one pass of the dovetail bit. A stop placed on the fence limits the length of the cut.

After cutting both ends of the top, I relocate the fence while the height of the bit remains constant. I extend the height of the fence to provide stability while cutting the hood sides. Using a piece of scrap pine the same thickness as the hood sides, I dicker with the fence until the joint is a firm press-fit. When satisfied, I cut the dovetails on the ends of the boards. Even though the dovetails extend across the entire width of the boards, the first inch closest to the front edge must be trimmed off for the rabbet cut into the inside faces of the sides.

THE FIT IS RIGHT. The mitered rabbet at each corner is a pleasing construction detail, and a practical means of building a door frame that will accommodate a piece of glass.

PROTECT THE CLOCK MOVEMENT FROM DUST

The rabbets cut into the inside faces on the sides have a double purpose. First, they act as a door stop, and second, they keep out dust, the main adversary of clock movements. I cut the rabbets in the same manner as I cut the ones in the clock case. Before gluing up the hood, I rout the front and ends of the top with the same roundover bit I had used on the case bottom.

The hood has no bottom, so for rigidity, I added a rail at the bottom of the hood behind the bottom door rail. I simply glue and nail the rail in place (see the drawings on pp. 104-105). The upper rail, located above the door, is cut to fit within the rabbets and also is glued and nailed in place. An inner rail is glued and nailed behind the upper rail to act as a dust stop. The three rails are taken from what's left after ripping the case sides.

HOOD DOOR IS RABBETED FOR A GLASS INSERT

The hood door is assembled with the ubiquitous mortise-and-tenon joint. Because this clock has only one door, and a small one at that, I cut the joints by hand. After cutting the door parts to size from the rippings left over from the case sides, I lay out the joint using a square and a marking gauge. I rout the edge with a ¼-in. roundover bit and cut the rabbet for the glass before cutting the joint.

The joint is easily cut by boring out the mortise with a brace and bit and then clearing out the waste with sharp chisels. I use a backsaw to cut the tenons on the ends of the rails, first making the cheek cuts and then supporting the rails in a bench hook to make the shoulder cuts.

Trimming the miters at the joints requires a mitering template to guide the chisel (see the left photo on the facing page). With the template cut to an accurate 45° and set at the layout line, it's a simple matter to cut a perfectly fitting miter (see the right photo on the facing page and the photo above). I make the door slightly oversized and trim it to a close fit after glue-up. Once I'm satisfied with the fit, I hang the door in the hood with simple butt hinges.

I bought the weight-driven, eight-day movement for this clock from Frei and Borel (126 2nd St., Oakland, CA 94607; 800-772-3456). It sits on top of a seat board made from three pieces of the wood I had left over. Appearing as the letter C sitting on its side, the seat board is attached to the ends of the case sides with dowels and without glue. Holes are bored into the seat for the pendulum as well as the weight chains. Another option would have been to extend the case sides and place a horizontal board bridging the sides where the movement would have been. The clock face, painted onto wood, is screwed to the seat board. The time ring on this dial is 7 in. dia. Paper dials are available from mail-order houses.

According to Kassay, the original clock was painted red, so I followed suit. I used Cranberry red paint available from Primrose Distributing (54445 Rose Rd., South Bend, IN 46628; 800-222-3092).

JOHN WILSON

Shaker Oval Boxes

A STACK OF FIVE SHAKER BOXES can be built in just a couple of days, even by novice woodworkers, as the author proves in his classes many times every year. The boxes are great for display or storage and make gifts that everyone loves to receive.

Oval boxes continue to be the most popular product the Shakers ever offered to the outside world. Originally produced for their practicality (nesting boxes inside each other required little storage space) and utility (almost anything and everything was stored in these durable containers), they have become collector's items for their simple beauty.

As testament to the boxes' enduring appeal, I've been able to make a living for the last 10 years by traveling around the country teaching Shaker box making to groups of woodworkers. Box making's appeal is that, in short order, you can have a stack of boxes, as shown in the photo at left, that any woodworker would be proud to show off or to give as gifts. In just a day and a half, my students, who range in ability from novice to advanced woodworkers, complete a stack of five traditional Shaker oval boxes.

The secret to the classes' efficiency is that we start with the tops, bottoms and band material thicknessed and rough dimensioned. I also bring the necessary patterns and forms for cutting the band's fingers, bending and drying the bands and shaping the tops and bottoms. I can supply all the necessary materials, hardware and forms if you want to make the boxes that way. But this article will show you how to prepare the stock and make your own patterns and forms.

There is no one right way to make an oval box, just as there is no one material for bands, no one system for numbering sizes of nesting boxes, nor one shape to the fingers. What can be said for the following procedure is that it works for me and for participants in my workshops to produce a stack of five boxes, from a small #0 to a #4 box, in the Shaker tradition. Because the #2 box is the mid-sized and easiest to work of the stack of five boxes, I suggest students start with it.

SELECTING AND PREPARING STOCK

Box bands for the base and the lid of an oval box are thin slices of hardwood, or thick veneers, that will bend and tack without splitting. The Shakers used maple bands and pine tops and bottoms more than anything else. But there are a wide range of hardwoods that are suitable for box making including ash, cherry, walnut, apple, hackberry, hard and soft maple and birch. Straight-grained wood is best for bending. Any wood can be used for the tops and bottoms.

I prefer quartersawn wood for both the bands and the tops and bottoms. In bands, the quartersawn grain reduces curling along the edges of the fingertips. Quartersawn wood is preferable for tops and bottoms because it has half the wood movement of flatsawn stock and is less likely to cause structural problems, especially in the larger sizes.

Moisture content also influences the workability and stability of the wood. Tops and bottoms should be dried to a moisture content (MC) of 8% to 9% to help prevent gaps showing up at the edges from shrinkage or splitting the band at the ends from expansion. Bands are easiest to work when air dried to 15% to 20% MC. Kiln drying band stock makes it brittle and more difficult to bend.

The thickness of the bands, tops and bottoms varies with each size box, as shown in the chart on p. 113. The most difficult part of preparing box stock is thicknessing band stock. Smaller boxes require thinner

bands to make the tighter radius bends, but the larger boxes need the heft of the thicker veneers.

When I first started making boxes, I resawed stock on my tablesaw. A sharp, carbide-tipped, 40-tooth blade yields a clean cut, and the 3-in. capacity of a 10-in. tablesaw is enough to cut bands for a #4 box in one pass. Tops and bottoms for up to a #4 box can be resawn by making a pass along each edge of the stock.

Most of the stock less than 0.10-in. thick that I use now is veneer-sliced to my specifications. These veneers are uniformly thick, and the knife leaves a smooth surface. But because the knife bends the wood during the cutting process, it can create checking in one side of the veneer. The checked side of the veneer will be more likely to split if placed on the outside of the box. The best way to determine the knife-checked face of veneer-sliced stock is to flex the band across its length in both directions. The side of the band that shows splitting or checking, as shown in the top photo on this page, should be used as the box's inside surface. Then bending will help control the splitting.

If a band does split while bending, you can still salvage the stock. Trim off the split edges and make a shallower box, often called a button box, or add a handle and make a carrier. The Shakers also had plenty of odd-sized boxes and carriers, although such boxes are less common.

PATTERNS, FORMS AND HOT-WATER TRAYS

I developed finger patterns and top and bottom oval patterns from drawings in *Measured Drawings of Shaker Furniture and Woodenware* by Ejner Handberg (Berkshire Traveller Press, Stockbridge, Mass., 1991). I then made permanent patterns from pre-painted aluminum coil stock used as trim by residential siding contractors for windows and doors. The coil stock cuts easily with a utility knife. Straight cuts are made by scoring the aluminum and then flexing it along the score. Curved lines can be scored freehand or cut with shears. I drilled

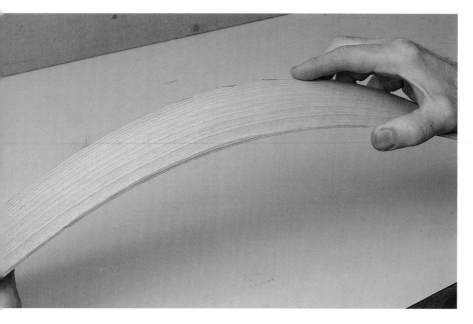

SPLITS OR CHECKS IN A VENEER FACE, caused by the veneer slicing process, are quickly revealed by flexing the band across its length. The split face should be to the inside of the box to prevent the splits from continuing along the grain line.

BEVELING THE FINGER EDGES AND ENDS is much easier if the band is first soaked in hot water and securely clamped to the bench. Reposition the hardboard cutting block for each finger set so that knife kerfs from previous cuts don't affect the cut.

$\frac{3}{64}$-in.-dia. holes to show where the copper tacks go.

Oval bottom patterns are made to the dimensions shown in the chart on p. 113. The top oval patterns are about $\frac{1}{8}$ in. larger. If you enlarge the bottom pattern by 2% on a copying machine, you will have a close approximation.

I use two different types of forms when making Shaker boxes. One form is the core around which I bend the bands, and the other form is the shaper that I plug into both sides of the bands for drying. By making up several sets of the shapers, I can mass-produce boxes with just one set of cores.

I made the cores out of pine or basswood, bandsawing them to rough shape and then disc or beltsanding them to refine the shape. The shapers are made from $\frac{1}{2}$-in.-thick pine for the #0 and #1 boxes and $\frac{5}{8}$-in.-thick pine for the #2 through #4 boxes. Use the same oval patterns as for the cores, but cut slightly outside the line at a 10° bevel. The shaper slides easily into the band, but the increasing diameter of the beveled edge stretches the oval band as the shaper is pushed deeper into the band. Two holes drilled through the shapers provide ventilation and a grip for pulling them out of the bands.

Another necessity for bending is a means of soaking the bands in hot water. I use a copper tray with a hinged lid, but a painted-steel window planter tray with a board on top also works well. Alternately, a vegetable drawer from an old refrigerator or a length of steel gutter with end caps and a plywood cover will do as well. An electric hot plate, as shown in the background of the photo at left on p. 111, works great for heating the water.

SHAPING THE FINGERS

Begin preparing the band stock by marking the finger pattern and tack locations, as shown in the drawing on p. 113, on the outside face of the band. Bandsaw the fingers along the layout lines to rough shape, and drill the $\frac{3}{64}$-in.-dia. tack pilot holes. Trim the fingers to finished form by clamping the band onto a Masonite cutting board and beveling the curved edge and end of each finger with a utility knife, as shown in the bottom photo at left. I find it much easier to make and control the cut if I soak the fingers in a glass of hot water for a few minutes first. Try to maintain the bandsawn shape, and keep the tip of the finger about $\frac{3}{16}$ in. wide. Note that the bevel is greatest at the bases of the fingers, about 20°, and decreases to about 10° at the tips.

The final step in preparing the band stock for bending is to feather the end of the band opposite the fingers. Tapering the last 1 in. to $1\frac{1}{2}$ in. of the band eliminates a bump inside the box where the band ends. I prefer to taper the band on a belt sander using a scrap of wood to apply even pressure to the band. If you don't have a belt sander, then you can handplane this taper.

BENDING THE BANDS

Some folks shy away from projects that involve bending because they think it is difficult. However, the thin band stock, aided by a good soaking in hot water, bends easily around the core. You'll want to have everything ready, though, so you can bend the band before it cools, which it will do in about half a minute.

I soak the bands in hot water (180° or hotter) for at least 10 minutes; 20 minutes will ensure that the troublesome bands are fully soaked (nothing is gained or lost after a half-hour). When ready, wrap the band around the core, making sure that the beveled side of the fingers faces out and

that the tack line is aligned with the center of the oval core. If, during the bending process, you notice the veneer splitting or feathering, as shown in the top photo on p. 110, stop. Turn the band inside out, rebevel the fingers, reheat the band and rebend it with the better side out. From this point until the band is tacked together, be sure to hold all the fingers all the time or the band is likely to split up the middle between the fingers.

With the band wrapped around the core and the tack line centered on the core, draw a register mark across the top edges of the overlapped section at the front of the band. This register mark lets you open the band to release the core and then to push the band back together into the same size oval shaped on the core. Hammer the copper tacks, and clinch them at the same time by nailing over a pipe anvil, as shown in the photo below right, to secure the fingers.

WHEN WRAPPING A BOX BAND around the core, be sure the beveled fingers face out and that the tack line is centered on the oval. An electric hotplate heats the copper tray in which the bands are soaked for about 20 minutes before bending.

TACKING BANDS WITH AN ANVIL BACKUP, clinches the tack. Once tacked, the top band will be dried in place on the box band. Shapers in the box band on the bench keep the band's oval shape while it dries.

The top band is made by repeating all the steps for the box band, except the box band is used instead of a core to bend the top band. After tacking the top band, slide it back on the box band to dry.

Let the bands air dry for two days before continuing. Oval shapers pushed into the top and bottom of the band will maintain their shape. You can speed up the process with a fan, but this can increase the edge curling around the fingers.

FITTING TOPS AND BOTTOMS

Before proceeding with the top and bottom, I like to sand the inside of the box and top bands with 120-grit sandpaper. I also make sure the ends of the bands feather well into the inside contours while it's still easy to get at these surfaces.

To mark the oval shapes for the tops and bottoms, you can make appropriate-sized patterns for each box size or you can use the bands themselves as patterns. It usually doesn't make any difference when making the bottoms because the shapers have made the bands oval. But the top bands have a bump in them where they were wrapped over the fingers of the box band. On the #0 through #4 boxes, a pattern-shaped top can even out the oval. On larger boxes, the band is thicker and doesn't stretch so easily. Therefore, on the larger sizes, using the band for a pattern gives a better fit.

Once the bottom is marked and roughly bandsawn to shape, the final fitting is done on a disc sander with the table set to bevel the edge 4°. The cork effect of the beveled edge provides a tight fit between the bottom and the band where the edge has been flared by the shapers. Check the fit frequently as you gradually sand to the line. The bottom should be snug but not overly tight.

Finger direction on a box is determined by the side of the band on which the bottom is fitted. Most boxes have fingers pointing to the right, although left-pointing fingers are not uncommon. Top band fingers always point in the same direction as the bottom band. Determine which direction you want your fingers to point, and insert the bottom by fitting it against the front lap of the band and into both ends; then stretch the back of the band over the opposite edge. Press the bottom into place until the entire rim of the band is slightly above the surface.

When the bottom is pressed firmly into place, lightly sand it level on the belt sander. Now you also have a good opportunity to hide any gaps between the bottom and the band. First work some glue into the gap, and then immediately sand the bottom, either on the belt sander or by hand. The sanding dust will mix with the glue to form a filler that blends perfectly with the box.

The bottom is held in place with square, wooden pegs (toothpicks) driven into predrilled pilot holes. Pilot holes are $\frac{1}{16}$ in. dia. for the #0 and #1 boxes and $\frac{5}{64}$ in. dia. for #2 and larger boxes. Drill holes equally spaced around the box, 2 in. to 3 in. apart, tap the pegs into the holes and snip off the ends with diagonal cutters. You can then sand the toothpicks flush or trim them with a utility knife.

The top is made following the same procedure as for the bottom. However, a loose-fitting top band can be snugged up by changing the shape of the top oval. Elongating the top oval will move the slack in the band to the ends of the oval, causing the band to hug the box in the middle for a positive friction fit.

FINISH THE BOX

Shaker boxes can be painted, varnished or oiled. Before the mid-1800s, the Shakers usually painted their boxes. In later years, they varnished them. I use a clear lacquer on my boxes after hand-sanding the outside with 120-grit paper. I first brush on a sanding sealer, followed by a coat of lacquer. Although many woodworkers like the ease of application of an oil finish, I don't like the odor that lingers for months inside the closed boxes. Lacquer and shellac also give the sharpest image to my favorite bird's-eye maple tops.

■ Shaker Oval Boxes

The dimensions of oval box components vary depending upon the boxes. The chart below provides dimensions for the five most popular sizes.

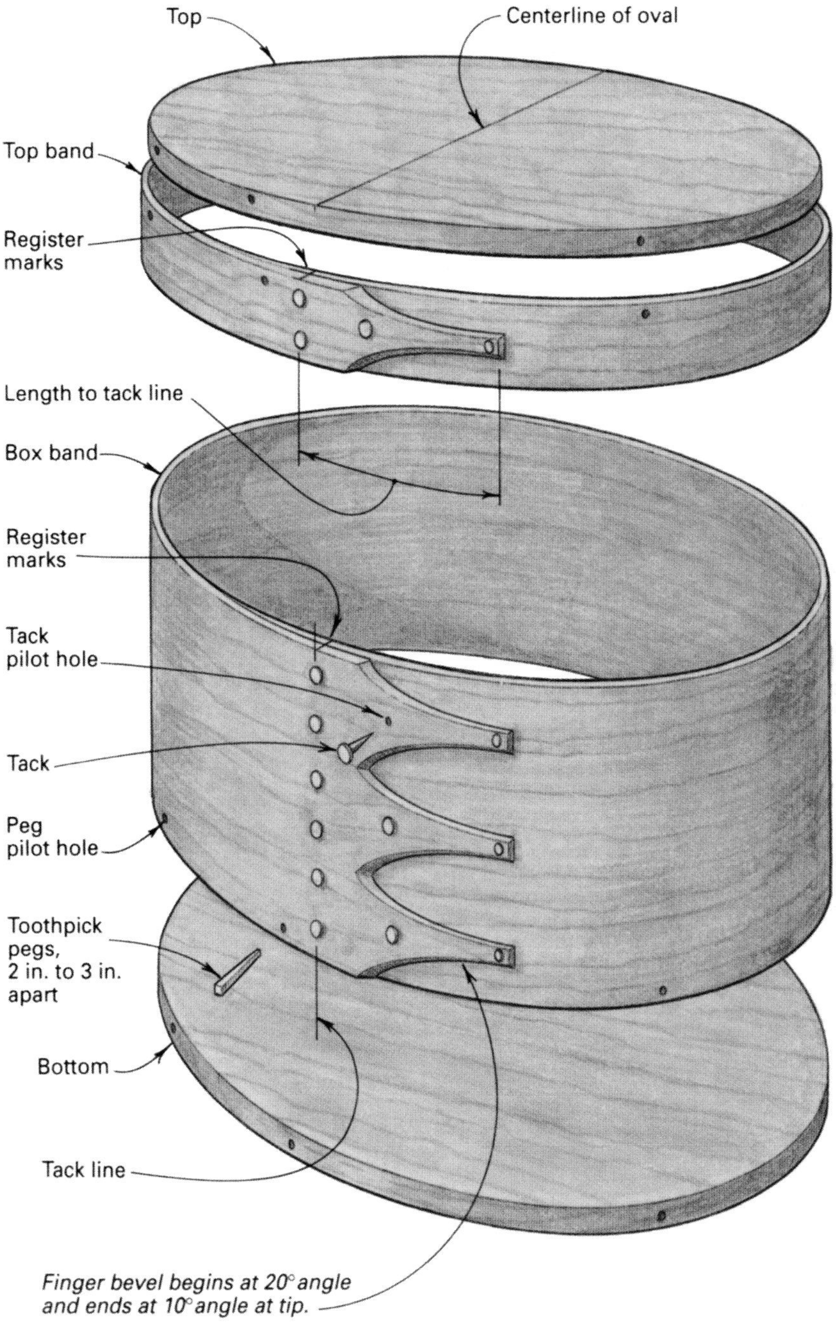
Top
Centerline of oval
Top band
Register marks
Length to tack line
Box band
Register marks
Tack pilot hole
Tack
Peg pilot hole
Toothpick pegs, 2 in. to 3 in. apart
Bottom
Tack line
Finger bevel begins at 20° angle and ends at 10° angle at tip.

OVAL BOX DIMENSIONS

Box size	Bottom oval* (WxL)	Top and bottom thickness	Box band (TxWxL)	Top band (WxL)	No. of fingers-length to tack line	Tack size
#0	1⅞ x 3½	0.195	0.060 x 1$\frac{1}{16}$ x 11⅞	$\frac{7}{16}$ x 12¼	2–1⅝	1 or 1½
#1	2$\frac{9}{16}$ x 4$\frac{9}{16}$	0.210	0.062 x 1½ x 15	½ x 15½	2–1¾	1 or 1½
#2	3½ x 5¾	¼	0.067 x 2 x 19	⅝ x 19¾	2–1⅞	1½
#3	4½ x 7	¼	0.072 x 2½ x 23	$\frac{11}{16}$ x 24	2 or 3–2$\frac{1}{16}$	1½
#4	5½ x 8¼	¼	0.077 x 3$\frac{1}{16}$ x 27	¾ x 28	3–2¼	2

* Top oval about ⅛ in. larger than bottom oval.

CHRIS BECKSVOORT

Molding that Stays Put

THIS MOLDING WILL LAST AS LONG AS THE CHEST. Applied over dovetailed keys, the molding will allow the case sides to move seasonally.

sk any antique collector or dealer about the most common problem with old case pieces and you're sure to hear a familiar refrain: The molding's always the first thing to go. Attaching molding to a solid carcase side is a problem. A wide case piece, such as a chest of drawers, can move ⅜ in. to ½ in. through the seasons as the ambient humidity rises and falls. Molding glued or nailed to the case sides, its grain perpendicular to the grain of the sides, isn't moving at all. There are two possible outcomes. Either the case sides will crack because the molding has prevented them from moving, or the molding will fall off because the side has moved and broken the glue bond between case side and molding.

I get around these problems by attaching side molding with a series of dovetailed keys (see the photo and drawing below). A dovetailed slot cut in the back of the side molding allows it to slide onto the short dovetailed keys attached to the case. The connection keeps the molding snugged up tight to the carcase. But because the mold-

ing is not glued to the carcase or to the keys, the case sides are free to move. This technique has been used for centuries and is still found on the highest caliber work. It takes a little extra effort to attach molding this way, but the molding will last as long as the case piece, and the case sides will not crack.

PREPARING THE CARCASE AND THE MOLDING

The case sides must be perfectly flat all the way across if the molding is to fit correctly. To check for flatness, I set the case on one side and hold a straightedge across the top edge of the exposed side. I pencil mark any high spots and beltsand the side flat. Then I flip the case over and repeat the process on the other side.

Once the case sides are flat, the front molding can be attached to the case. I miter one end of the front molding, position it in place and mark the other end. After cutting the second miter, I glue the molding to the

Attaching moldings with dovetailed keys

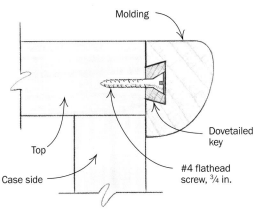

Dovetailed keys, spot glued and screwed to the carcase, secure the molding snugly without restraining movement.

ROUT THE DOVETAILED SLOT IN TWO PASSES. Start the slot in the molding with a straight bit; then make a second pass with a dovetail bit set to full-depth.

ROUT THE DOVETAILED KEYS. Use a piece of scrap to set the fence on the router table, making adjustments until the key fits snugly into the molding slot.

front of the case. The grain direction of the molding is the same as the case, so wood movement isn't a problem.

Routing the dovetailed slot in two passes

I rout the dovetailed slot in the two pieces of side molding in two passes on my router table. I remove the bulk of the slot with a straight bit. For the second pass, I use a ½-in.-wide dovetail bit set to full-depth, about ¼ in. for the 1⅛-in.-high molding I used on this chest (see the top photo at left). On smaller case pieces, I use a molding that's ⅞ in. high and rout a ⅜-in.-wide slot, also ¼ in. deep. For either size molding, I position the dovetailed slot just a little bit higher than the center of the molding, so it's not weakened excessively.

When I have finished routing slots in both side pieces (and in some extra stock, just in case), I check the depth with a dial caliper. This depth reading gives me the precise thickness for the dovetailed keys. Be sure to check it in several places along each piece of molding. The depth can vary slightly if pressure on the moldings isn't absolutely consistent when routing the slots. I generally don't find variations of more than 0.005 in., which is not a problem. I just thickness the keys to the shallowest reading taken with the dial caliper (see the photo on the facing page). If there's more variation than 0.005 in. overall, I'll re-rout new molding.

MAKING THE DOVETAILED KEYS

I make the keys from a blank that's a little thicker than ½ in., about 3 in. wide and a few inches longer than the case sides. Before cutting the keys for the case, I use a piece of scrap of the same thickness to make a test piece, adjusting the fence on the router table until the fit is snug but non-binding. I rout a dovetailed profile onto both sides of the blank, top and bottom (see the bottom photo on the facing page). Then I saw off the keys with a little to spare.

Keys are taken to final thickness in a planer. Because the keys are so thin, I use an auxiliary bed to prevent snipe. I take material off the narrower side of the keys, checking the thickness with a dial caliper after each pass. The keys should be between 0.003 in. and 0.005 in. thinner than the slot depth, so the molding will be pulled tightly to the case.

ATTACHING THE KEYS AS CONTINUOUS STRIPS

A series of keys, not one long piece, holds each side molding to the case sides. But if installed as separate keys, alignment could be a real headache. Instead, I attach the keys as one continuous strip on each side of the case and then chop out the waste between individual keys, which are glued and screwed to the case. This allows the case sides to move and ensures that all the keys are in line, making it much easier to slide the molding home.

PLANE THE KEYS TO THICK-NESS. Check with a dial caliper after each pass. Keys should be .003 in. to .005 in. thinner than the slot is deep.

TACK KEYS IN PLACE. A dab of glue and a brad at the center of each key hold the strip in place.

The first step in attaching the keys is positioning them. I hold a strip of molding against the side of the case, with the top edge of the molding flush with or just slightly proud of the top of the case (it's easier to remove a little bit of molding than it is to level the whole top down to the molding). With a knife, I mark both the top and bottom of the dovetailed slot, at the front and rear of the case. Then I connect these marks using a straightedge. I now have the position of my key strip.

The next step is to lay out where the keys will be and where waste will be removed between them after the key strip has been attached. Because I've built quite a few of these five-drawer chests, I have a pattern. I made the pattern by marking out the center of the key strip, and then dividing each half into three keys separated by ½-in. spaces. I marked for screws about ⅛ in. to either side of the centers of the individual keys.

I put a dab of glue at the center of each of the marked keys and then tack the strip with some ¾-in., #20 brads (see the photo above). I countersink holes for the screws that ultimately hold the keys in place and

drive home the ¾-in., #4 screws by hand (see the top photo on the facing page). The waste between the keys is chopped out with a chisel and a mallet (see the bottom photo on the facing page).

EASING ASSEMBLY

I take just a sliver off the leading edge of each key and the dovetailed slot in the molding, so the molding will slide home more easily. Then I lubricate the inside of the dovetailed slot with a bit of graphite by rubbing the sides and bottom of the slot with a No. 2 pencil. Keep it back at least 2 in. from the miter, where the molding will be glued.

I test the fit of the molding, sanding the tops of the keys slightly if they seem too tight. The molding should slide right onto the keys without binding. After testing the fit, I put a dab of glue on the miter and on the first 2 in. of the case and then tap the molding home. I clamp the molding across the case at the miter. After the glue has dried, I saw off the excess at the back of the case.

COUNTERSINK HOLES, AND THEN SCREW THE KEYS DOWN. A little beeswax applied to the screw threads will make the job easier and reduce the chance of a screw breaking.

CHOP OUT THE WASTE. The author uses a mallet and a sharp chisel to remove waste between keys. Any chisel marks between keys will be hidden by the molding.

GLENN A. CARLSON

Weaving Shaker Tape Seats

I make Shaker chairs for a living. I also serve as the resident chairmaker at Hancock Shaker Village in Pittsfield, Mass., where I periodically teach people to weave chair seats. My students are often surprised to discover how easy the technique is to master.

The early Shakers made their chair tape from wool. Later, they switched to cotton. I prefer cotton tape to other woven seat material because it's durable, comfortable, easy to apply and available in a variety of colors. (Two sources of cotton tape are Connecticut Cane and Reed, 860-646-6586, and H. H. Perkins, 800-462-6660.) This is the same material that the military uses for belts and backpack straps, so it's durable.

THE TOOLS ARE BASIC

You can weave a seat with only a few basic tools (see the photo on p. 122). You may already have most of them in your shop. There are likely to be two exceptions: a steel surgical clamp and a wooden weaving needle. You could weave a seat without either of these tools, but they'll make the job a lot easier.

The surgical clamp, also called a hemostat, is a cross between a pair of scissors and a Vise-Grip. You can use it to grab and pull the cotton tape, or you can double the tape over the nose of the tool and push it

through a tight space. You should be able to buy one at a surgical-supply or a fish-tackle shop for $5 to $10. A wooden needle also can be used to thread the tape. I fabricated mine from a discarded chair slat.

WRAP THE WARP FIRST

Applying Shaker tape is relatively simple. First you wrap one piece of tape around the seat rungs from front to back. This is called the warp. On an average-sized chair, the warp is approximately 20 yds. long. The second piece of tape, called the weft, is woven through the warp from side to side. When weaving two colors of tape, always use the darker color for the warp because it covers the front rung where the seat will soil the most.

To calculate length, wrap the tape around the seat frame, front to back, one full revolution, and mark that length on the bench. Measure the distance between the back posts, or legs. If you're using ⅝-in.-wide tape, every 5 in. of rung will need eight rows of tape to cover it. For 1-in. tape, every inch of rung equals one row of

NEW AND OLD. The new chair seats in the forefront were woven by the author; the older chairs behind them are from the collection at the Hancock Shaker Village in Massachusetts.

EVERYTHING YOU NEED TO WEAVE A SEAT. Most of what you see here are basic shop tools, except the wooden weaving needle and the surgical clamp.

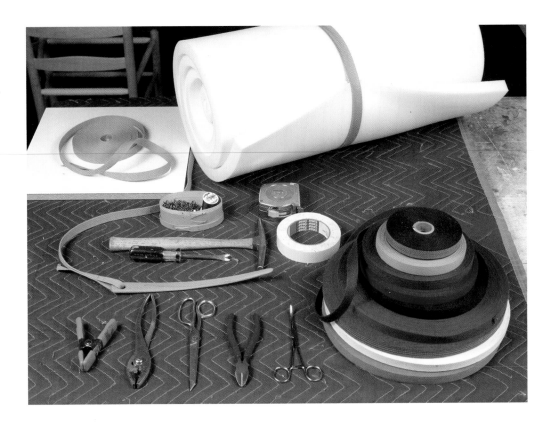

tape. Pull the required amount of tape from a roll, adding an extra row or two to be safe.

Tack one end to the seat frame at the back of the left side rung, using no. 3 upholstery tacks, ⅜ in. long (see the photo #2 on p. 124). I always drive tacks into the rungs on the inside edge so the metal heads won't wear through the cloth tape over time. Bring the tape around the front rung, under the bottom and back up over the top of the back rung.

Repeat this process a few times, wrapping loosely. Then pull all the excess through. Keep wrapping this way until you use up most of the material. Before wrapping the last row or two, clamp the tape to the front rung, and then go back to the first row and pull each row tightly enough to take up the slack (see photo #4 on p. 125). Later, the weaving process will tighten the warp more. Use your fingernails and a tack

puller (with sharp edges filed dull so they won't tear the cloth) to compress each row slightly between the back posts. Add an extra row or two if you have the room, but don't overlap the material. Turn the chair over, and tack the material to the side rung near the back post (see photo #5 on p. 125). Cut off any excess.

Because the chair seat is wider at the front, you'll have to fill in the triangular gaps at the front corners of the frame (see photo #6 on p. 124). Use short pieces, 1 or 2 ft. long, and tack each piece to the side rungs, top and bottom. Start each piece at the top, and finish it on the bottom, as much toward the back as possible. It makes no difference if the number of filler strips is the same on each side. What counts is that the wood rungs are covered with the cloth tape. Be sure to compress the tape to fit in as many rows as possible.

FILL THE CENTER WITH FOAM

Cut a 1-in.-thick, high-density foam pad slightly smaller than the seat frame, and push it into the space between the top and bottom layers of the warp (see photo #7 on p. 124). Choose an opening roughly one-third of the way across the seat. Use one hand to push the foam into place and the other hand (on the underside of the seat) to help pull it along. The foam acts as a cushion and helps the top and bottom layers of tape work together to support a load.

WEAVE THE WEFT LAST

Start the weaving with one long piece of tape, called the weft, that stretches between the left and right rungs of the chair frame (see photo #8 on pp. 124-125). Calculate the yardage you'll need using the method of wrapping and measuring described for the warp piece. Always add an extra row or two for good measure. Because the seat frame is larger at the front, the test wrap should be measured a little front of center so the calculated length will not be too short.

To weave in the weft, start at the back of the chair and work forward. But before beginning the weaving process, place a piece of cloth-backed, double-faced tape along the back two-thirds of each side rung. This will prevent the Shaker tape, over time and use, from sliding backward on the trapezoid-shaped seat frame. Pull the backing paper off gradually as you weave toward the front of the seat to expose more adhesive. The Shakers solved this problem by gluing cloth to the side rungs. The cloth was part of a packet filled with straw or wood shavings designed as a cushion. I don't think they'd object to using foam and double-faced tape instead.

With the chair upside down on the working surface, feed one end of the tape in from the right side, under two widths of cotton tape in the warp and then over two. You'll end at the left rear corner. Tack the new length of tape under the existing warp piece to the back rung in the left rear corner.

Turn the chair upright. Thread all the material through your hands to find the top and bottom of the tape so that you don't get it twisted. Weave the first row on the top of the chair seat, under two, over two. Flip the chair, and weave through the bottom layer. Turn the chair upright again. Be sure to tuck the end of the tape into the seat to make it ready for the next layer of weaving. Then pull the long length of tape all the way through. The waxed paper backing on the double-faced tape will make the Shaker tape slide more easily.

Using the tack puller and your fingers, straighten the row, and push it toward the back of the chair seat. Pull the Shaker tape tightly, removing any slack, and secure it to the double-faced tape.

Continue weaving the seat toward the chair front. Weave over the tacks holding the warp filler strips in place. Weave under the filler strips as soon as you can because that will help to strengthen the weave.

If you need to fit one more row when you reach the front of the seat and it appears there's not enough room for a width of tape, simply compress the last six or eight rows with your fingers. Turn the chair upside down, pull the final length of weft through at the front corner, and tack it to the front rung, under the warp (see photo #10 on p. 125).

1. MEASURING TAPE LENGTH. The author first wraps a piece of the cloth tape one full revolution, front to back. Then he measures the distance between the back posts to calculate the number of rows that will fit over the back rung.

2. ONE TACK SECURES THE WARP. The warp is one continuous piece of cloth tape stretched over the front and back rungs of the chair seat.

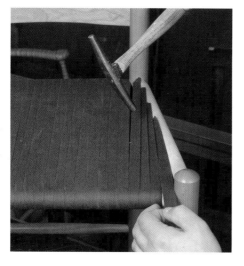

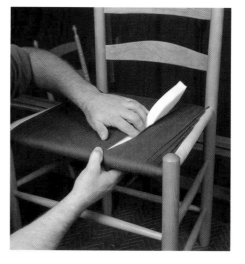

8. THE WEFT IS NEXT. After weaving the tape front to back, the author adds the weft the side-to-side rows. He starts at the back of the chair.

6. FILL IN THE CORNERS WITH SHORT PIECES. The chair seat is wider at the front, so the triangular gaps on either side must be filled in with separate pieces of tape.

7. THE FOAM SERVES A DUAL PUR-POSE. It cushions the seat for a softer feel, and it strengthens the two layers of tape so that they stretch as one when weighted down.

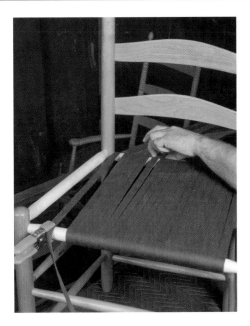

3. ROWS DO NOT OVERLAP. Each row of tape should butt firmly to the one next to it. No wood should show through when the seat is done.

4. GETTING RID OF SLACK. The author clamps the end of the warp in place. Then he goes back to the first row to pull the tape securely. After that, he pulls the rows tightly to one another and adds another row or two to cover the back rung.

5. TACK THE END OF THE WARP to the underside of the side rung, near the back. The goal is to hide all the tacks from view when the seat is finished.

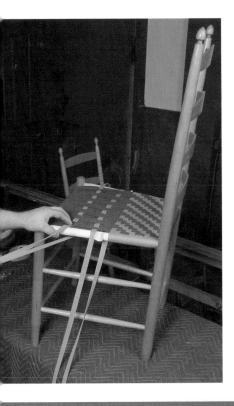

9. SURGICAL CLAMP REACHES INTO TIGHT SPACES. It can be used to push or pull the tape. Doctors use this tool, so do fly fishermen. A clamp costs less than $10.

10. END THE WEFT ON THE BOTTOM. One tack to the underside of the front rung, after all the rows have been pulled tightly and adjusted for neatness, finishes the job.

Inspiration

Your workshop is a creative outlet. Sometimes you want to make simple projects, sometimes elaborate, and sometimes you're just not sure. That's where this section comes in. You'll find a variety of examples here to inspire you. Specifications and design information help you make the leap from inspiration to reality.

GLENN A. CARLSON

Slat-Back Armchair

A DESIGN DERIVED FROM THE SHAKERS. This four-slat armchair, based on Shaker chair designs of the late 19th century, is sized to suit 20th-century bodies and carrier shipping requirements.

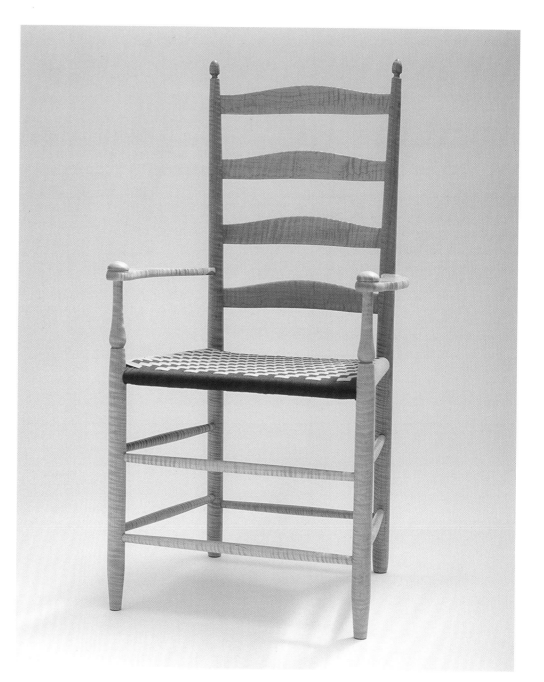

In the 1870s, Brother Robert Wagan began mass-producing chairs at the Shaker community in Mt. Lebanon, New York. His guidance brought uniformity and standardization to Shaker chairmaking. Although the lines of my chairs are unmistakably Shaker, they are not identical.

One difference is the number of slats, the horizontal members between the two back posts. Shaker chairs like this one originally would have had only three slats. My chairs have slightly higher backs and include four slats because that design looks more pleasing to my eye and because customers seem to prefer it. I have also added a little bit of height to the seat because people are physically larger now than they were 100 years ago and a higher seat height is more comfortable. The chairs fit in a box that just meets UPS shipping requirements—a 20th-century design constraint.

Back posts and slats are shaped by first steaming them in a homemade steam box and then bending them on fixtures fashioned after the ones the Shakers used. Stretchers connecting the four posts lock together mechanically inside the posts to make the chairs stronger and less liable to come apart. I use 100% cotton webbing in contrasting colors in the woven seat. Each seat requires about 45 yd. of the material.

While I do not work from the religious impulse that motivated the Shakers, I do strive to honor their aim for perfection, lack of ornamentation and simplicity of line.

THE WEBBING IS AUTHENTIC. Cotton webbing in contrasting colors is what a Shaker chairmaker would have used to weave a seat.

■ Interlocking Stretcher Tenons

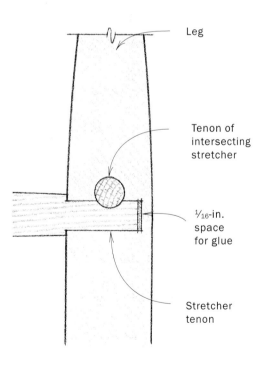

Leg

Tenon of intersecting stretcher

1/16-in. space for glue

Stretcher tenon

SPECIFICATIONS

■ DIMENSIONS
23 in. wide, 19 in. deep, and 41 in. high.

■ MATERIALS
Tiger maple and cotton webbing.

■ FINISH
Hand-rubbed tung oil with wax topcoat.

ERIC GESLER

Shaker-Inspired Corner Table

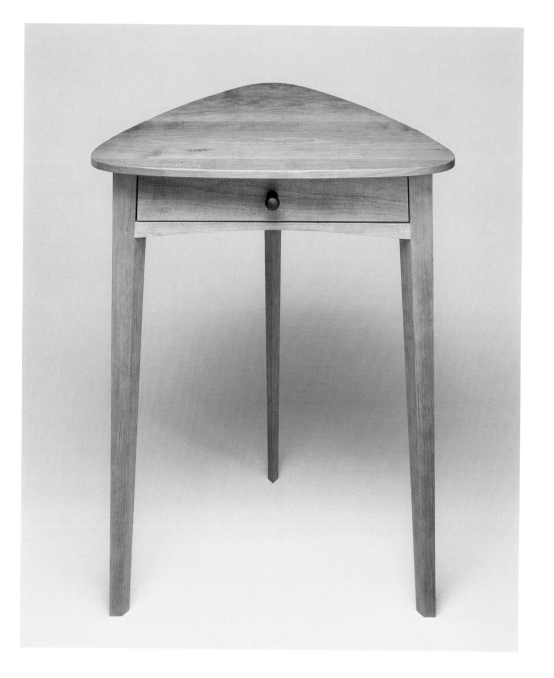

SHAKER TABLE WITH A TWIST. The rounded corners on the top, the curved front apron and the diamond-shaped tapered legs add a little bit of elegance to a simple form.

approached the design of this table from the top down, beginning with an equilateral triangle and then rounding the corners.

Once I felt comfortable with the triangular shape of the top, I drew the top view of the legs and the apron to figure out the shapes and the joinery involved. I wanted the legs and the apron to be flush, so I decided that it made sense for the legs to be diamond-shaped. I made a mockup of a tapered, diamond-shaped leg to get a feel for the proportions and to see how the leg profile changed, depending upon the vantage point.

At this stage I decided a drawer would give the table more visual interest. Having the drawer swing rather than slide gives it a fun and novel element. I used the top view I had drawn to decide how the swing on the

drawer would work. During construction, I decided to add a small rabbet at the bottom of the drawer, making the reveal consistent.

Finally, in keeping with the thin, tapered legs, I chamfered the underside of the top to make it look lighter. Most traditional corner tables I've seen have sharp corners and hard edges. I wanted something softer, friendlier, with the versatility to be used anywhere in the room.

SPECIFICATIONS

■ DIMENSIONS
21½ in. wide and 27 in. high.

■ MATERIALS
Cherry, pine and ebonized cherry pull.

■ FINISH
Boiled linseed oil, satin urethane and turpentine mixture, and wax.

I decided to make the drawer on my "Shaker-Inspired Corner Table" (p. 130) pivot open, rather than pull out like a standard drawer. I started by drilling a ¼-in. hole through the front left corner of the drawer where I wanted it to pivot, and then I positioned the drawer in the table to mark where the dowel enters the lower apron and top (see drawing below).

This design is fairly straightforward, except for one problem. Because one end of the dowel is held in place by the top, any movement of the top due to moisture will throw off the careful fit of the drawer. The drawer is flush with the apron and has a uniform reveal; a change in the position of the dowel would make the fit look sloppy and might impede the smooth action of the pivot.

To prevent this, I used a combination of dowels and screws to fasten the tabletop to the base. Two dowels, drilled into the two front legs, hold the front edge of the top in place. I used elongated screw holes along the two sides, which allow the top to expand and contract toward the back of the table, leaving the front—and the drawer—locked firmly in place. A block attached to the side of the triangular drawer acts as a stop, keeping the drawer from pulling out or going in too far (see photo above).

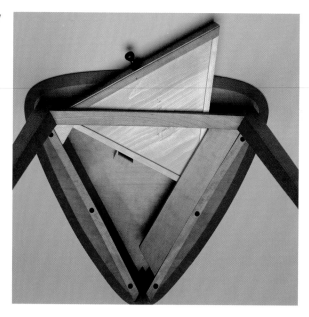

SNUG FIT. This triangular drawer pivots on a dowel. The block attached to the side acts as a stop for both opening and closing.

■ A Triangular, Pivoting Drawer

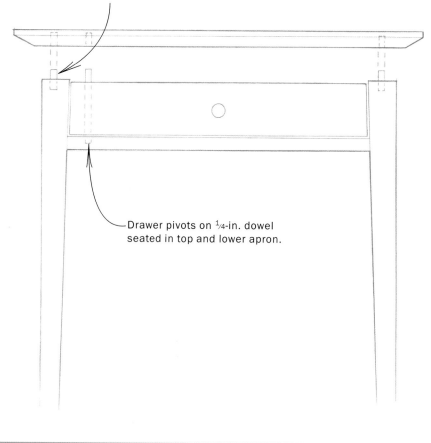

Dowels from front legs into top allow wood movement from front to back.

Drawer pivots on ¼-in. dowel seated in top and lower apron.

PETER TURNER

Cherry Side Table

Shaker craftsmen had an eye for beauty and function in the furniture they made. I expressed that appealing combination, paying particular attention to proportion and simple details. The table is sized to flank my sofa at home, with the height of the table matching that of the sofa arm.

I kept the top and the shelf fairly thin to lighten the overall appearance of the table. The top's ample overhang allows a large work area while keeping the base fairly light. I had seen a turning detail that I liked for the leg and found a drawing of it in one of Ejner Handberg's books of shop drawings (*Shop Drawings of Shaker Furniture and Woodenware*, The Berkshire Traveller Press, 1975). The leg has a long, square section at the top and a graceful barrel shape below.

Breadboard ends on the top and the shelf provide stability and isolate the legs from any seasonal movement in the shelf. The shelf allows my wife and me to clear the tabletop of clutter in seconds. But its location near the top of the table doesn't detract from the table's overall proportions.

JOINERY IS TRADITIONAL, TOO. Half-blind dovetails on the drawer and pinned tenons connecting aprons and legs were signature details of Shaker furniture. They still work.

SPECIFICATIONS

■ DIMENSIONS
26½ in. long, 18⅛ in. wide, and 26½ in. high.

■ MATERIALS
Cherry with hard maple drawer sides and runners.

■ FINISH
Polymerized tung oil.

SHAKER ORIGINS. A simple turned leg, a thin top and wide overhangs help define the Shaker style. Splayed legs give the table a confident stance, and the shelf makes the table practical.

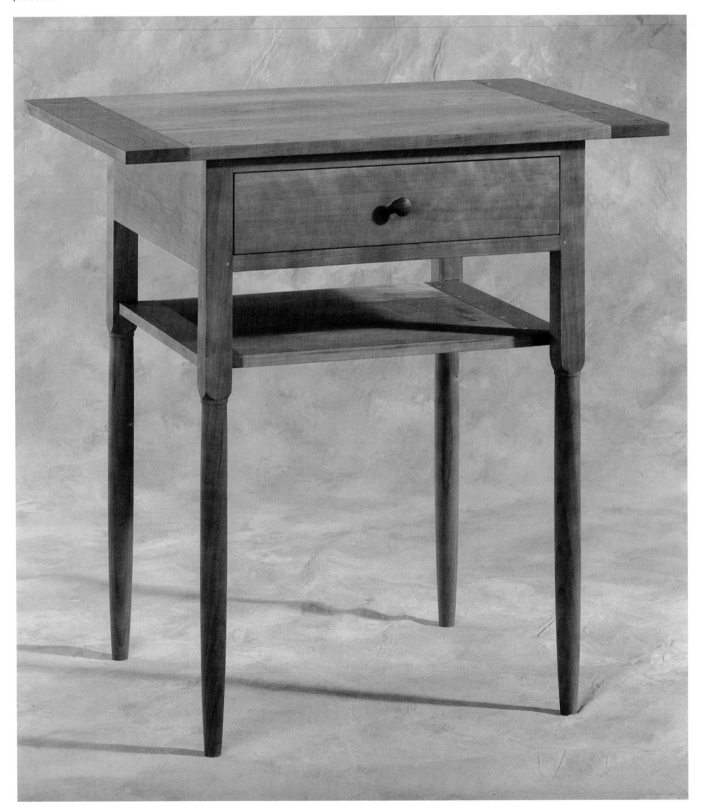

SHELF FOR A SIDE TABLE

The Shaker-style side table I made is a lot more practical because of its broad shelf. It provides a second top. The breadboard ends, which are pinned to the shelf, gave me a way to hang it without worrying that the seasonal cross-grain movement of the wood might break the legs or crack the joinery in the frame (see drawing below).

I left the breadboard ends of the shelf long enough so that the excess could be trimmed into tenons. The tenons fit into mortises cut on the inside edges of the legs. Because wood expands and shrinks across the grain a great deal more than it does along the length of the grain, the dimensions of the shelf where it intersects the legs won't change much. Had I not used a breadboard end on the shelf, but just a solid panel of wood, the table eventually would have come to grief.

If you try this, make sure the breadboard piece is wide enough so that the joint between the end and the shelf panel is set inside the leg. That way the panel won't push into the leg as it expands with high humidity.

■ Making a Stable Shelf

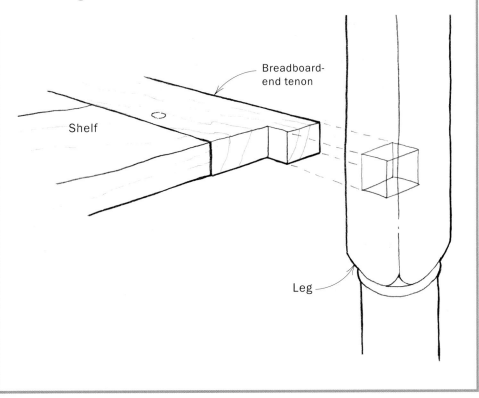

Breadboard-end tenon

Shelf

Leg

CEES OTTE

Dining Table in the Shaker Style

My rather shabby pine table needed to be replaced. But the new table had to be cat-resistant. My feline companions were the main causes of the demise of the old table. For the new table I decided to try hard maple because I guessed it was hard enough to resist the cats' nail sharpenings and because the color was in the same range as European pine.

At first, I was inclined to copy a Shaker table from a photograph or a book. But on second thought, none of those designs was exactly to my liking. I found the Shaker style very attractive, though, so I opted to draw a table of my own design in a similar style.

SHAKER STYLING SUITS MODERN DINING. The maker designed this table to seat up to eight people. Its drawers hold utensils for all of the place settings.

DIVIDED DRAWER WON'T FALL OUT. Extra-long sidepieces on the table's two drawers allow easy access to all of the compartments.

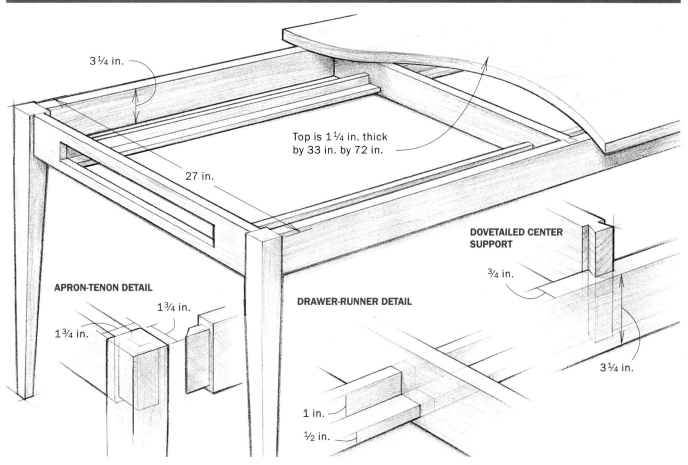

3¼ in.

Top is 1¼ in. thick
by 33 in. by 72 in.

27 in.

**DOVETAILED CENTER
SUPPORT**

¾ in.

APRON-TENON DETAIL

1¾ in.

1¾ in.

DRAWER-RUNNER DETAIL

¾ in.

3¼ in.

1 in.

½ in.

The top, at 1¼ in., is thicker than many Shaker tops I had seen, and the 3¼-in.-wide aprons are narrower. The table had to seat six people with ease and eight maximum. I also wanted the table to have drawers because I like to have the cutlery at hand when I'm setting the table. I placed a drawer at each end of the table, and I made one drawer with dividers for silverware.

I bought the wood in Amsterdam at one of the wood wharves, a sort of lumberyard at the docks. I had the wood dimensioned at a carpenter's shop because I have a small shop with no room for big surfacing machines.

The tabletop is glued up from four boards and has breadboard ends. To accommodate wood movement, I attached the top to the aprons using wooden buttons, and I connected the breadboard ends using thick splines, glued only at the middle. The table frame has mortise-and-tenon joinery.

The drawers use half-blind dovetails at the front and full dovetails at the back. What's unusual about the drawers is their length. The drawers are as long as about half the table's length, or roughly 32 in., with the divided portion at the front and a bottomless part at the back. This allows the drawer to be pulled out far enough for access to all of the silverware bins, and strips of wood screwed to the underside of the top prevent the drawers from dropping very far.

SPECIFICATIONS

■ **DIMENSIONS**
72 in. long, 33 in. wide, and 29 in. high.

■ **MATERIALS**
Hard maple.

■ **FINISH**
Linseed oil, turpentine and beeswax.

METICULOUS DOVETAILS.
Because the maker likes traditional joinery and tools, he cut dovetails by hand.

Shaker Collector's Cabinet

This 15-drawer cabinet was originally built for a collector who wanted "lots of different-sized drawers." It is strongly influenced by Shaker design: lack of molding, graduated flush drawers, mushroom knobs, and the only ornamentation is in the figure of the cherry. Even the size is reminiscent of a dwarf clock built by Brother Benjamin Youngs, Sr.

Its aesthetic simplicity belies its inner complexity. Technically, it is a fairly demanding piece. It has 170 individual parts, with 296 hand-cut dovetails, fully mortised and tenoned telescoping web-frames between the drawers and a flush two-panel back. The back is finished so that the cabinet can be used as a freestanding piece and enjoyed from all sides. The top and all drawer fronts and cabinet sides are cut from one board. There are two secret compartments, and as with all my pieces, I hid a silver dollar from the year of construction somewhere inside.

SHAKER INSPIRED. This 15-drawer collector's cabinet is narrow enough to fit into small spaces, and it exhibits the spareness and lack of ornamentation of Shaker furniture.

This is a cabinet built to function smoothly and to last. Potential wood movement is taken into consideration at every stage of construction. The front base inset, for example, follows the grain direction of both sides and the bottom. Each drawer is carefully sized to allow for expansion, no matter what the season or the location. The drawers are fully finished and waxed, and slide smoothly, as if on glides.

All this adds up to a diminutive piece of technical perfection, an interesting cabinet in which to store treasures.

SPECIFICATIONS

■ DIMENSIONS
14 in. wide, 15 in. deep, and 50 in. high.

■ MATERIALS
Black cherry.

■ FINISH
Linseed oil.

ALL-AROUND BEAUTY.
The flush two-panel back is finished so that the cabinet can be used as a free-standing piece.

OUTER PLAINNESS, INNER COMPLEXITY. This simple-looking cabinet has 170 pieces, put together with 296 hand-cut dovetail joints. The drawers are carefully sized to accommodate seasonal wood movement.

THOM DUPREX

Shaker-Style Apothecary Chest

FINDING A NEW FUNCTION. The apothecary chest was used in pharmacies for storing small items. The author used the form to make a quilter's work table.

This apothecary chest was designed as a sewing storage chest and work table. It provides a large work surface at a comfortable height with plenty of convenient storage.

As the name suggests, the apothecary chest was a staple in old pharmacies. It often had rows and rows of differently-sized drawers in which a pharmacist kept all his powders and chemicals. Those cabinets are things of the past, but the name has survived and remains a common description of a chest with a lot of small drawers.

I decided to use this form for a sewing chest in part because my wife, Faith, had taken up quilting and needed small storage spaces. She suggested a large, walk-around sewing surface at standing height with lots of drawers (she not only stands to cut fabric but prefers to sew standing up). I adapted the design (mostly the drawer configuration) from a 19th-century Shaker apothecary chest. The piece is a utilitarian success not only for quilting but also for stashing yarns, crochet cotton, embroidery floss, stencils and patterns.

The chest is unmistakably Shaker in pedigree, and I used highly figured bird's-eye maple to give its plain form some distinction. Because the piece was designed to be placed away from the wall, I used bird's-eye maple panels on the back as well. Graduated drawer sizes (and pulls) provide vertical balance, which I thought would be important on such a wide chest.

I used bird's-eye maple veneer over a medium-density fiberboard substrate for the

PULLS GROW WITH THE DRAWERS. The turned cocobolo drawer pulls are graduated in size vertically, as are the drawers.

side and back panels. The top is also veneered and surrounded by a solid maple frame. Using veneered rather than solid panels made it easier to match the figure and added strength and stability. The drawer fronts and corner posts are solid maple.

VENEER MAKES IT STABLE. Using veneered panels instead of solid adds stability and allows the maker to consistently match the striking bird's-eye figure.

SPECIFICATIONS

- **DIMENSIONS**
  55¾ in. wide, 26 in. deep, and 36 in. high.

- **MATERIALS**
  Maple, bird's-eye maple veneer, poplar, and cocobolo.

- **FINISH**
  Shellac and varnish.

JAMES DeSALVO

Entertainment Center

Faced with severe space constraints, my clients had searched in vain through commercial furniture sources for an entertainment center that would satisfy their needs. They had lots of electronic equipment, including a television, a VCR, a turntable, a tuner, a tape deck, a CD player, a cable box and switch box, not to mention CDs, videotapes and audio cassettes, that they wanted to fit into the cabinet. Yet the space available for an entertainment center to house all this equipment was less than 3 ft. wide.

Price was important, so I concentrated on finding the right balance between fine furniture and production furniture. The result was this Shaker-style cherry cabinet. I used dowels to create a strong carcase with simple joinery. Because this was a limited production piece, I wanted to work as efficiently as possible, so I used the same thickness stock whenever possible to minimize milling and increase yield.

Simple frame-and-panel construction keeps production costs low. To give the case some substance, I used raised panels. But to get the flat, recessed look typical of many Shaker pieces, I put the raised portion of the panel inside the cabinet. The panels fit into rabbets in the frame and are held in place with wood strips. This allows panels to be stained and finished prior to final assembly.

I used ½-in. thick cherry-veneered plywood for the top and the back panel. The back panel has a full-length cutout for ease

A BACK PANEL WITH A FULL-LENGTH CUTOUT
makes it easy to connect all the electronic components in the cabinet. A slightly larger hole behind the television lets it protrude slightly through the cabinet back.

of wiring. The full-length retractable doors ride on rack-and-pinion type hardware to eliminate any racking when sliding the doors in or out. The bottom drawer and the turntable shelf pull out on full extension slides, and the television sits on a heavy-duty pullout swivel shelf. Included is storage for 120 CDs and more than 36 videotapes and audio cassettes.

SPECIFICATIONS

■ DIMENSIONS
    35 in. wide, 21 in. deep, and 76 in. tall.

■ MATERIALS
    Cherry and cherry-veneered plywood.

■ FINISH
    Oil finish with a light stain.

CONVENIENT STORAGE on roll-out shelves and drawers is accessible behind fully retractable doors. This unit houses nine electronic components.

PAULA GARBARINO

Entertainment Center on a Tight Budget

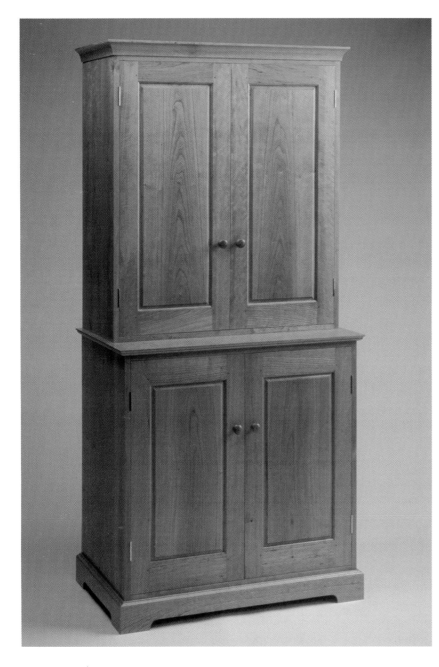

Three constraints led to the design of this cabinet: First, it needed to be in keeping with the traditional Cape Cod house for which it was planned. Second, the cabinet had to hold a 26-in. television, but the visual bulk had to be reduced as much as possible. Third, it couldn't be expensive. So to come in on budget, I needed to rely on familiar techniques and minimal hand-work (I used store-bought pulls) without compromising the joinery.

A TV cabinet in the Shaker style may seem incongruous, but that style satisfied all three of these design requirements, and most important, it suited the client's taste.

I started by designing solid-wood cases with dovetail joinery for the upper and lower cabinets. The upper case, which is shallow and slightly taller, counterbalances the bulk of the lower case. This is a common trick in traditional furniture design,

SPECIFICATIONS

■ DIMENSIONS
36½ in. wide, 23¾ in. deep, and 77¼ in. high.

■ MATERIALS
Cherry.

■ FINISH
Shellac sealer, Waterlox, and butcher's wax.

and it is used to good effect in large pieces, such as secretaries, highboys and various kinds of display cabinets. By putting the large television in the lower case, I could make the upper case only 17 inches deep.

I gave the door frames a coped, molded inner edge, and I cut the door rails from the same board to get continuous figure. The solid-wood panels are bookmatched and float in grooves. The cornice profile was cove-cut on a table saw. The alternative—making or buying shaper knives—would have added cost to the project.

The lower unit has a slide-out shelf for the television and a shelf for a VCR; the upper case holds a tuner, a CD player and a slide-out shelf for the turntable. The drawers hold CDs, and the space above is for record storage. The plywood back has openings for wiring and ventilation.

AARON HILTEBEITEL

A Shaker-Inspired Cupboard

■ Cupboard with Shaker Roots

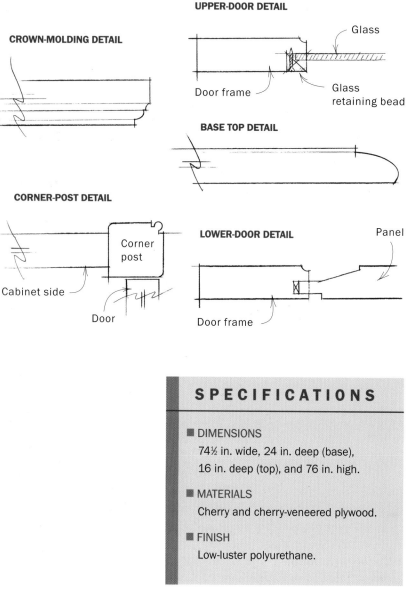

UPPER-DOOR DETAIL

Glass

Door frame

Glass retaining bead

CROWN-MOLDING DETAIL

BASE TOP DETAIL

CORNER-POST DETAIL

Corner post

Cabinet side

Door

LOWER-DOOR DETAIL

Panel

Door frame

SPECIFICATIONS

■ DIMENSIONS
74½ in. wide, 24 in. deep (base),
16 in. deep (top), and 76 in. high.

■ MATERIALS
Cherry and cherry-veneered plywood.

■ FINISH
Low-luster polyurethane.

I designed this cupboard in a Shakerish style but added some decorative details, such as raised panels, and curved lines for a little flair. The curves and the large, open serving area help lighten the overall appearance of the piece. The two wide drawers at the bottom of the cupboard provide storage for table linens.

I selected solid cherry for all exposed surfaces on the basis of its figure and color match. The interior of the cabinet is made of cherry-veneered plywood so that wood movement would not be a problem. The top and the base were built as two separate units so that the cupboard would be easier to move.

European hardware was my choice for hanging the doors and the drawers. This hardware works well and imparts a quality feel to the piece. Also, this style of hardware is easy to install and adjust. But the thing I like most about European hardware is that it doesn't show on the front of the cabinet, leaving an ultra-clean look with uninterrupted lines.

THIS CHERRY CUPBOARD combines traditional Shaker styling with curved lines and a large, open center serving area for a light and airy effect.

CHRIS BECKSVOORT, author of *The Shaker Legacy*, gardens, teaches, writes, snowshoes, and bicycles in New Gloucester, Maine. In real life he designs and builds furniture.

STEVEN THOMAS BUNN owns and operates a one-man shop in Bowdoinham, Maine. He specializes in crafting traditional Windsor chairs to his own design, as well as creating licensed reproductions for two museums. His chairs can be seen at www.windsorchairresources.com/bunn.html.

JEAN M. BURKS is the curator of decorative arts at Shelburne Museum in Shelburne, Vermont. She has worked at numerous museums and written for many magazines on topics ranging from brass candlesticks to Shaker sweaters.

GLENN A. CARLSON owns Shaker Chairs, a one-man shop in Norfolk, Connecticut, specializing in the construction, restoration and repair of Shaker chairs. He also works two days a week at nearby Hancock Shaker Village, where he demonstrates seat-weaving techniques.

JAMES DeSALVO has run an architectural millwork shop since 1980 in Brewster, New York. Five employees help him produce kitchen cabinets, vanities, and library shelving. In 1992, he started another company specializing in high-quality production furniture.

THOM DUPREX runs a one-man shop in northern New Hampshire building furniture in Shaker and 18th Century Philadelphia styles. He emphasizes traditional hand techniques, and has devoted extensive time to developing carving skills by working with Master Carver Dimitri Klitsas.

PAULA GARBARINO taught Furniture Making at North Bennett Street School for five years. She has since moved back to full-time shop work, making furniture.

ERIC GESLER works at Dana Robes Wood Craftsmen in the Enfield Shaker Village in New Hampshire, where he is Chief Designer and Director of Woodworking Instruction.

GARRETT HACK opened his own shop in 1973 and later studied furnituremaking at Boston University's Program in Artisanry. He designs and builds furniture in Vermont and is a regular contributor to *Fine Woodworking* magazine. He is the author of *The Handplane Book* and the upcoming *Classic Hand Tools*.

AARON HILTEBEITEL works with Classic Restorations in Massachusetts. He does layout and fabrication of in-house casework, room layout and coordination, finishing, and carpentry.

IAN INGERSOLL designs and builds furniture in West Cornwall, Connecticut.

CEES OTTE is a hobbyist woodworker who lives in the Netherlands, making furniture for himself and his friends. He occasionally sells a piece. He taught himself woodworking by trial and error, and by watching a friend whose father is a furnituremaker.

TIM RIEMAN is a furniture maker who builds reproduction Shaker furniture. He is the co-author of *The Complete Book of Shaker Furniture*.

MARIO RODRIGUEZ is a consultant to Lie-Nielsen Toolworks. He is also a teacher and the author of *Traditional Woodwork*, as well as a contributing editor for *Fine Woodworking*.

ROBERT TREANOR lives in San Francisco, where he builds Shaker furniture and writes about woodworking.

PETER TURNER builds custom furniture in Portland, Maine.

JOHN WILSON is a Shaker box maker, instructor and supplier of parts, hardware and related tools in Charlotte, Michigan.

CREDITS

Vince Babak (illustrator): 30–31, 33, 129

Christopher Clapp (illustrator): 42–45

William Duckworth (photographer): 41, 122

Harvey Edwards (photographer): 128

Charley Freiberg (photographer): 140–141

Zachary Gaulkin (photographer): 74, 76–77

Michael Gellatly (illustrator): 16–19

Scott Gibson (photographer): 21–23, 25, 27, 28 (bottom), 31–32, 100–101 (large), 102, 104–105

Dennis Griggs (photographer): 66, 78, 114, 138–139

Dennis and Diane Griggs (photographers): 29 (bottom table photo)

Boyd Hagen (photographer): 130–132

Hancock Shaker Village, Hancock, Mass. (photograph): 8 (right)

Aaron Hiltebeitel (illustrator): 146 (original drawings)

Sloan Howard (photographer): 129

John Keith Russell Antiques, South Salem, N.Y. (photograph): 12 (bottom)

Susan Kahn (photographer): 108

Henkjan Kamerbeck (photographer): 136–137

Jefferson Kolle (photographer): 99 (bottom)

Heather Lambert (illustrator): 57, 113

Bob La Pointe (illustrator): 48–49, 52, 63, 69, 70–71, 78, 80–81, 83–84, 87–88, 96–98, 103, 107, 137

Vincent Laurence (photographer): 62, 65, 68, 70, 72–73, 80, 82, 115–119

Peter Macomber (photographer): 28 (top two table photos), 133–134

Robert Marsala (photographer): 43–46, 55

Steve Morse (photographer): 144–145

Michael Pekovich (illustrator): 115

Scott Phillips (photographer): 15, 18–19 (furniture courtesy Hancock Shaker Village, Pittsfield, Mass.); 34–37

Putnam Photo (photographs): 142–143

Jay E. Reed (photographer): 147

Jim Richey (illustrator): 75, 77

Timothy Rieman (photographer): 7, 9 (top left, bottom), 10 (right), 11, 13 (left), 24

Charley Robinson (photographer): 56, 58–59, 85, 89–90, 110–111, 120–121, 124–125

Mark Sant'Angelo (illustrator): 135

David A. Schorsch (photographer): 12 (top)

John Sheldon (photographer): 61

Skinner, Inc., Boston, Mass. (photograph): 8 (left), 9 (top right), 10 (left), 13 (right)

Robert Treanor (photographer): 50 (bottom)

Kaz Tsuruta (photographer): 47, 101 (right)

Peter Turner (illustrator): 37

Rosalie Vaccaro (illustrator): 146 (renderings)

Marc Vassallo (photographer): 93–95, 97–98, 99 (top)

Alex Waters (photographer): 50 (top left, top right), 51, 53

METRIC EQUIVALENCE CHART

Inches	Centimeters	Millimeters	Inches	Centimeters	Millimeters
⅛	0.3	3	12	30.5	305
¼	0.6	6	13	33.0	330
⅜	1.0	10	14	35.6	356
½	1.3	13	15	38.1	381
⅝	1.6	16	16	40.6	406
¾	1.9	19	17	43.2	432
⅞	2.2	22	18	45.7	457
1	2.5	25	19	48.3	483
1¼	3.2	32	20	50.8	508
1½	3.8	38	21	53.3	533
1¾	4.4	44	22	55.9	559
2	5.1	51	23	58.4	584
2½	6.4	64	24	61.0	610
3	7.6	76	25	63.5	635
3½	8.9	89	26	66.0	660
4	10.2	102	27	68.6	686
4½	11.4	114	28	71.1	711
5	12.7	127	29	73.7	737
6	15.2	152	30	76.2	762
7	17.8	178	31	78.7	787
8	20.3	203	32	81.3	813
9	22.9	229	33	83.8	838
10	25.4	254	34	86.4	864
11	27.9	279	35	88.9	889
			36	91.4	914